ALSO BY JULIA CHILD

Mastering the Art of French Cooking, Volume I
(with Simone Beck and Louisette Bertholle)

The French Chef Cookbook

Mastering the Art of French Cooking, Volume II
(with Simone Beck)

From Julia Child's Kitchen

Julia Child & Company
(with E. S. Yntema)

Julia Child & More Company
(with E. S. Yntema)

The Way to Cook

Cooking with Master Chefs

In Julia's Kitchen with Master Chefs
(with Nancy Verde Barr)

Julia and Jacques Cooking at Home
(with David Nussbaum)

These are Borzoi Books, published in New York by Alfred A. Knopf.

Julia's Kitchen Wisdom

Julia's Kitchen Wisdom

ESSENTIAL TECHNIQUES AND RECIPES
FROM A LIFETIME OF COOKING

by Julia Child

WITH DAVID NUSSBAUM

ALFRED A. KNOPF

NEW YORK 2000

THIS IS A BORZOI BOOK
PUBLISHED BY ALFRED A. KNOPF

Copyright © 2000 by Julia Child

All rights reserved under International and Pan-
American Copyright Conventions. Published in
the United States by Alfred A. Knopf, a division
of Random House, Inc., New York, and
simultaneously in Canada by Random House
of Canada Limited, Toronto. Distributed
by Random House, Inc., New York.

www.aaknopf.com

Knopf, Borzoi Books, and the colophon are
registered trademarks of Random House, Inc.
Companion to the television special
produced by A La Carte Communications

Library of Congress Cataloging-in-Publication Data
Child, Julia.
Julia's kitchen wisdom : essential techniques and
recipes from a lifetime of cooking / by Julia Child
with David Nussbaum.
p.   cm.
ISBN 0-375-41151-8
1. Cookery. I. Nussbaum, David. II. Title.
TX651 .C523 2000
641.5—dc21   00-062928

Manufactured in the United States of America
First Edition

Contents

Illustrations follow pages 36 and 68

Acknowledgments

This book represents some forty years of happy collaboration on cookery with colleagues and friends. The idea for it came when we decided to make a television special out of snippets from my earlier shows starting with the very first one, "Boeuf Bourguignon," that famous French beef stew, which aired February 11, 1963, on Boston's "educational" station, WGBH. You can't have a food show without a book to go with it—hence this volume. It is with deepest appreciation that I acknowledge the following angels who made it all possible.

My continuing gratitude goes to Judith Jones, who has been my editor since the beginning of my cookbook life. Hers is the conception of this book, and it is she who carefully went over each suggestion, each chapter and paragraph, yes, and even each sentence. Her remarks and suggestions are golden, and her advice is treasured. My admiration of Judith as an editor and my affection for Judith as a person are boundless.

David Nussbaum, my collaborator, has done a magnificent job of gathering and sifting through material from all the various shows and books. He has done testings and comparisons, made outlines and suggestions, and always presented me with detailed material eminently ready to work on. The book, literally, could not have been done at all, and certainly not by the deadline, had it not been for David.

My special thanks go to Geoffrey Drummond, producer of the two-hour PBS television special *Julia's Kitchen Wisdom* that gave rise to this book. Geof and his editor, Herb Sevush, went through miles of old tape to pick out just the right episodes to show, and then edited them all into a lively whole. Geof's company, A La Carte Communications, Inc., with Nat Katzman, also produced my last four series, *Cooking with Master Chefs, In Julia's Kitchen with Master Chefs, Baking with Julia,* and *Jacques and Julia Cooking at Home,* as well as two *Cooking in Concert* PBS specials with Jacques Pépin. Segments from all of these shows appear in the present special. We have always had a great time working together, and my admiration and affection for Geof are infinite.

Continuing and enthusiastic thanks to Public Television for making my career possible. I simply would not have existed without them, and I very much appreciate the support and the freedom that PBS offers its participants. How lucky we are that it exists!

Sincere thanks to many who have helped me through the years and whose work has meant much to the success of our TV special as well as to the recipes in this book: William A. Truslow, Esq., my family lawyer and faithful friend. Russell Morash, my first producer, who started us out on *The French Chef* and kept us going through the *Julia Child & Company* series; and Marian Morash, The Victory Garden Cook and our first executive chef. Ruthie Lockwood, sometime producer of *The French Chef,* unique personal director, and valued friend. Rosemary Manell, talented food designer for photography as well as television, and recipe developer for many of the shows and books. The wonderfully talented Sarah Moulton, sometime executive chef on our *Company* series. Stephanie Hersh, my longtime assistant and friend, without whom my office would be a mess and my life both dull and in disarray.

A project of this magnitude cannot happen without the support of generous sponsors, and this is particularly true of Public Television. I am proud that we are associated with the Robert Mondavi Winery, whose pioneering spirit and generosity have made California wines recognized throughout the world. I am delighted, too, that my favorite spread, Land O' Lakes Butter, is with us again—we used an incredible 573 pounds of it on our *Baking with Julia* series. And much of that good butter finds its way into the pots and pans of All-Clad Metalcrafters, our final sponsor. Heartfelt thanks to you, all three.

Toujours bon appétit!

Introduction

So often you can be in the midst of cooking and you just can't remember whether that leg of lamb should roast in a 325° or a 350°F oven, and for how long. Or you've forgotten just what you do to unmold a jelly-roll cake, or the system that so successfully brings back the hollandaise sauce. This book aims to give quick, snappy answers to many of those questions.

It won't by any means answer everything, and it doesn't go into such complicated subjects as French puff pastry, for which you need pages of instruction and numerous photographs. In other words, it doesn't pretend to take the place of a big, detailed, all-purpose cookbook like my *Way to Cook* or *Mastering the Art of French Cooking*, Volumes I and II. It is, rather, a mini aide-mémoire for general home cookery, and is aimed at those who are tolerably familiar with culinary language; whose kitchens are normally well equipped with such staples as jelly-roll pans, a food processor, a decent rolling pin; and who know their way around the stove reasonably well.

It began as my loose-leaf kitchen reference guide gradually compiled from my own trials, remedies, and errors—corrected as I've cooked my way through the years. Now that it has evolved into a book, information is arranged according to the large categories of soups, eggs, bread, and so forth, with the emphasis on technique. Whether a crêpe is rolled with mushrooms for a main course or with strawberries for dessert, all crêpe dishes are made in much the same way, so they are all together in one chapter. The same goes for soufflés, tarts, meats, and the rest of the menu. In the roasting section, for instance, the master recipe, though brief, details the technique for dealing with a large piece of meat. Here the master recipe is for roast beef, and is followed by still briefer variations for other roasts such as leg of lamb, roast chicken, turkey, fresh ham, and even a big whole fish. They all cook in essentially the same way, though small details differ. The same is true for soufflés and tarts; and green vegetables are grouped in two convenient charts according to method. Once you have mastered a technique you hardly need look at a recipe again, and can take off on your own.

If you have watched the PBS television special that was the inspiration for this book, you will note that the recipes demonstrated there are included here but that the method or ingredients are often not quite like those on the screen. Many of those recipes were conceived years ago. Take the garlic sauce for mashed potatoes as an example. That was a good system for its time, but an involved one. Here it is much simpler and equally good, if not even better.

A thorough professional index is essential for this kind of book. When you have a question, for instance, just look it up by subject, such as "Chocolate, about melting," or "Mayonnaise, about troubleshooting," or "Sole Meunière," or "frying pans," and so forth. My own little loose-leaf served me well, and I am hoping this book version will give you, too, as well as me, many of the essentials needed for brief instruction and problem solving.

Julia Child
Cambridge, Massachusetts

Julia's Kitchen Wisdom

Soups and Two Mother Sauces

"Once you have mastered a technique, you hardly need look at a recipe again."

Homemade soups fill the kitchen with a welcome air, and can be so full and natural and fresh that they solve that always nagging question of "what to serve as a first course."

PRIMAL SOUPS

These are the basic soups, the least complicated, and often the most loved.

MASTER RECIPE

Leek and Potato Soup
For about 2 quarts, serving 6

3 cups sliced leeks (white and tender
    green parts; see box)
3 cups peeled and roughly chopped "bak-
    ing" potatoes
6 cups water
1½ tsp salt
½ cup sour cream or *crème fraîche* (see
    box, page 9), optional
    Bring ingredients to the boil in a 3-quart saucepan. Cover partially and simmer 20 to 30 minutes, until vegetables are tender. Correct seasoning. Serve as is, or purée (see box, page 4), and/or top each portion with a dollop of the cream.

VARIATIONS

▮ ONION AND POTATO SOUP. Substitute onions for leeks, or use a combination.

▮ CREAM OF LEEK AND POTATO SOUP. After simmering the preceding soup, purée it (see box, page 4) and whisk in ½ cup heavy cream. Reheat to the simmer again before serving.

▮ WATERCRESS SOUP. Add a bunch of washed watercress leaves and stems to the base soup for the last 5 minutes of cooking. Purée. Garnish with a scattering of fresh watercress leaves.

▮ COLD SOUPS, such as vichyssoise. Purée any of the above, stir in ½ cup cream, and chill. Correct seasoning just before serving; stir in chilled cream if you wish. Top each bowl with minced fresh chives or parsley (or fresh watercress leaves).

■ SOUPE DU JOUR. Meaning add anything else you have on hand, such as cauliflower, broccoli, green peas, spinach, cooked or raw. This is how you may come up with some of your own marvelous ideas and secret "house recipes."

HOW TO PREPARE LEEKS. Trim off the root ends, keeping the leaves attached. Cut off tops so the leeks are 6 to 7 inches long. Starting ½ inch from the root and keeping leaves attached, slit each leek lengthwise in half and then in quarters. Wash under cold running water, spreading the leaves apart to rinse off all dirt. Leeks can be braised whole (page 33) or sliced crosswise into pieces for soup. To julienne, cut leeks crosswise into 2-inch pieces, press leaves flat, and slice lengthwise into matchsticks.

TO PURÉE A SOUP. To use an immersion blender, set the machine upright in the center bottom of your soup pan, turn it on and move it around, but do not bring it to the surface. To use the food processor, strain the soup and turn the solids into the processor, adding to them a little of the liquid, then process, adding a little more liquid as needed. To use the vegetable mill, strain the soup and add the solids gradually to the mill, passing them through with small additions of the liquid.

STOCKS

Light Chicken Stock

Bring to the simmer in water to cover a collection of raw and/or cooked chicken bones, trimmings, gizzards, and necks (but no livers). Skim off scum that rises to the surface for several minutes, then salt very lightly. Cover loosely and simmer for 1 to 1½ hours, adding water if needed. You may also wish to include chopped onions, carrots, celery (½ cup each for every 2 quarts of bones), and an herb bouquet (see box, page 58). Strain and degrease.

To make a "strong chicken stock," boil it down to concentrate its flavor.

When the stock is cool, cover and either refrigerate for several days or freeze.

■ TURKEY, VEAL, OR PORK STOCK.
Proceed as for the light chicken stock,
above.

■ HAM STOCK. For 2 quarts of ham
bones and scraps, include 1 cup each
of chopped carrots, onions, and celery,
and an herb bouquet (see box, page 58)
consisting of 3 imported bay leaves,
1 teaspoon thyme, and 5 whole cloves or
allspice berries. Proceed as for the
chicken stock, but simmer about 3 hours.

■ BROWN CHICKEN, TURKEY, OR
DUCK STOCK. Chop the bones and
scraps into ½-inch pieces and brown in
hot oil in a frying pan, and for every 2
quarts of them add ½ cup each
chopped carrots, onions, and celery
stalks. When nicely browned, transfer
to a heavy saucepan. Skim fat out of
frying pan, pour in cup of dry white
wine, and scrape coagulated browning
juices into it, then pour into the
saucepan, adding chicken stock and/or
water to cover ingredients. Include an
herb bouquet (see box, page 58), salt
lightly, and cover loosely. Simmer,
skim, strain, and degrease as for the
light chicken stock.

Simple Beef Stock

Arrange a collection of meaty raw
and/or cooked beef bones, such as
shank, neck, oxtail, and/or knuckle, in a
roasting pan, adding (for every 2 to 3
quarts of bones) ½ cup each of roughly
chopped onions, celery, and carrots.
Baste lightly with vegetable oil and
brown for 30 to 40 minutes in a 450°F
oven, turning and basting with oil or
accumulated fat several times. Scoop
bones and vegetables into a stockpot.
Pour fat out of roasting pan and deglaze
with 2 cups of water, simmering and
scraping up coagulated juices. Pour into
pot, adding cold water to cover ingredients by 2 inches. Add more chopped
onion, celery, and carrot (½ cup each
for every 2 to 3 quarts of bones), a
chopped fresh tomato, 2 large cloves of
smashed unpeeled garlic, and a
medium herb bouquet (box, page 58).
Bring to the simmer, skim off scum for
several minutes, and continue as for the
preceding chicken stock, but simmer 2
to 3 hours.

■ BROWN VEAL, PORK, OR LAMB
STOCK. Proceed as for beef stock, above,
but omit the carrots for lamb stock.

Fish Stock

Wash fresh fish frames (bones and
head, minus gills) from lean white fish
such as cod, hake, flounder, halibut,
sole. (Do not add dark skin.) Chop into
pieces. Bring to the simmer in a large
pot with water to cover by 1 inch. Skim
off scum for a few minutes, salt lightly,

cover loosely, and simmer 30 minutes. Strain. Boil down to concentrate flavor. Cover when cool, and refrigerate for a day or freeze.

USING CANNED BROTHS AND BOUIL-LONS. To disguise your use of the can, simmer the broth for 15 to 20 minutes with a handful of minced carrots, onions, and celery and perhaps a bit of dry white wine or dry white French vermouth.

NOTE: I use the terms broth and bouillon interchangeably, whether fresh or canned; stock refers to homemade.

COOKING WITH OR WITHOUT WINE. For red wine, use a young, full wine such as a zinfandel or a Chianti. White wines should be dry and full-bodied, such as a sauvignon, but because many of the whites are too acid, I prefer to use a dry white French vermouth. In addition to its strength and quality, it keeps nicely. Port, Madeiras, and sherries must be dry. If you do not wish to cook with wine, simply omit it, or add stock or more herbs.

SOUPS MADE FROM STOCK OR CANNED BROTH

MASTER RECIPE

Chicken Soup with Vegetables
For about 2½ quarts, serving 6 to 8

8 cups chicken stock (page 4) or canned
   chicken broth
1 imported bay leaf
½ cup dry white wine or dry white French
   vermouth
1 cup each julienne or fine dice of onion,
   celery, white of leek, and carrot
2 boned and skinned chicken-breast
   halves
Salt and pepper

Bring stock or broth to the simmer with the bay leaf, wine, and vegetables; simmer 5 to 6 minutes, or until the vegetables are just tender. Meanwhile, cut the chicken into thin slices, and the slices into julienne matchsticks 1½ inches long. Fold them into the soup and let simmer just a minute or two, until cooked through. Correct seasoning, then let sit for 15 to 20 minutes, allowing the chicken to absorb flavors. Serve hot with melba toast or buttered toast points.

■ BEEF AND VEGETABLE SOUP. In a large saucepan, sauté 1 cup each finely diced onion, celery, carrot, and leek for 2 minutes in butter. Pour in 2 quarts beef stock (page 5) or canned bouillon. Add ½ cup diced turnip; ½ cup orzo (rice-shaped pasta), quick-cooking tapioca, or rice; and, if available, any cooked and chopped beef shank or oxtail meat left from making beef stock. Simmer 10 minutes. Meanwhile, blanch for a minute or so 1½ cups shredded green cabbage leaves; drain, chop, and add to soup with ¾ cup peeled, seeded, diced tomato (see box, page 30). If you've not used meat, add also ¾ cup cooked or canned red or white beans. Reheat to the simmer for a few moments; season to taste, and serve.

■ FRENCH ONION SOUP. In a large saucepan, slowly sauté 2 quarts thinly sliced onions in 3 tablespoons butter and 1 of oil for about 20 minutes, until softened. Stir in ½ teaspoon each salt and sugar; sauté 15 to 20 minutes more over moderate heat, stirring frequently, until golden brown. Sprinkle 2 tablespoons flour over onions and cook slowly, stirring, for 2 minutes. Off heat, whisk in 2 cups hot beef stock or canned beef broth and ¼ cup cognac or brandy. When well blended, stir in 2 quarts more stock or broth and 1 cup dry white wine or dry white French vermouth. Simmer, loosely covered, for 30 minutes. Season to taste, and serve.

■ ONION SOUP GRATINÉE. Line the bottom of a large casserole or individual crocks with hard-toasted French-bread rounds (see box); top with thin slices of Swiss cheese. Ladle the hot onion soup over them, float more toast rounds on top, and cover with a layer of grated Swiss or Parmesan. Bake in a 450°F oven 20 minutes, or until cheese is melted and browned.

HARD-TOASTED FRENCH-BREAD ROUNDS—*CROÛTES.* For about 18, made from a 16-inch baguette. Slice the bread ¼-inch thick and dry out for 25 to 30 minutes in a 325°F oven, until light brown and crisp. You may wish to paint them with olive oil halfway through.

Mediterranean Fish Soup

For about 3 quarts, serving 8. Sauté 1 cup each sliced leeks and onions in ¼ cup olive oil until almost tender. Stir in 2 or more large cloves of chopped garlic; 3 cups peeled, seeded, and roughly chopped tomatoes (see box, page 30); a tablespoon of tomato paste; 2 pieces dried orange peel if available; and ½ teaspoon each dried thyme and fennel seeds. Simmer another 5 minutes. Pour in 2 quarts fish stock (page 5) or light chicken stock. Stir in a pinch of saffron if available. Season lightly, and bring to the boil; simmer for 20 minutes. Mean-while, make a *rouille* (red garlic sauce; see box), and cut into 2-inch chunks 3 pounds (6 cups) of skinless and boneless lean fish, such as cod, halibut, sea bass, monkfish. When almost ready to serve, add the fish to the soup, bring to the boil, and cook a minute or so, just until fish turns opaque and is springy to the touch. Spread the *rouille* on hard-toasted French-bread rounds (see box, page 7) and place in soup bowls. Ladle on soup and fish, sprinkle with chopped parsley and grated Parmesan cheese, and serve, passing more *rouille* separately.

ROUILLE—RED GARLIC SAUCE. To accompany fish soups, boiled potatoes, eggs, poached fish, pastas—and for all garlic lovers. In a heavy bowl, purée 6 to 8 large minced cloves of peeled garlic to a fine paste with ¼ tsp salt (see box, page 34). Pound in 18 large leaves fresh basil, chopped; ¾ cup lightly pressed-down fresh bread crumbs (see box, page 46); 3 tablespoons soup base or milk. When paste is smooth, pound or beat in 3 egg yolks. Switch to an electric mixer and beat in ⅓ cup diced canned red pimiento, and by driblets, as for making mayonnaise, ¾ to 1 cup fruity olive oil, to make a strong, thick sauce. Season with salt, pepper, and Tabasco.

AÏOLI. Omit the pimiento here, and you have the famous garlic sauce, aïoli.

Scotch Broth

For about 2 quarts, serving 6. Bring 2 quarts lamb stock (page 5), or lamb stock plus chicken broth, to the simmer. Stir in ½ cup barley, lentils, or almost cooked white beans (or add canned beans later), and ½ cup each diced onion, turnip, and carrot. Fold in 1 cup peeled, seeded, and diced tomato (see box, page 30). Cover loosely and simmer about 15 minutes, until vegetables are tender; season to taste. Stir in 3 tablespoons chopped parsley, and serve.

CREAM SOUPS

MASTER RECIPE

Cream of Mushroom Soup
For about 2 quarts, serving 6

4 Tbs butter
1 cup minced onion or white of leek
¼ cup flour
1 cup hot chicken stock (page 4)

6 cups milk
1 quart fresh mushrooms, trimmed, washed, and diced
¼ tsp dried tarragon leaves
½ cup or more heavy cream, sour cream, or *crème fraîche* (see box, page 9), optional
Salt and freshly ground white pepper

Drops of lemon juice, optional
Sprigs of fresh tarragon or slices of
    sautéed fresh mushroom caps,
    for garnish

The Soup Base. Sauté the onion or leek slowly with the butter in a heavy-bottomed covered saucepan, for 7 to 8 minutes, until tender and translucent. Blend in the flour and cook slowly 2 or 3 minutes, stirring. Off heat, gradually whisk in the hot stock. Bring to the simmer over moderate heat, and whisk in the milk.

The Mushrooms. Blend in the mushrooms and dried tarragon, and simmer 20 minutes, stirring frequently to prevent scorching. Stir in optional cream, simmer briefly, then season to taste, adding drops of lemon juice if needed. Garnish with tarragon sprigs, or with sautéed mushroom slices floated on each serving.

CRÈME FRAÎCHE—FRENCH SOUR CREAM. This is unpasteurized heavy cream allowed to ferment naturally. You can simulate it either by blending 1 tablespoon of sour cream into a cup of heavy cream and allowing it to ferment and thicken at room temperature, or by whisking together equal amounts of sour cream and heavy cream until thickened. The cream will keep for a week under refrigeration.

TO KEEP CREAM SOUPS AND SAUCES. To prevent a skin from forming on the surface of flour-thickened soups and sauces, stir them up every few minutes.

Or, to keep longer, float a film of milk or stock on the surface by filling a large spoon with the liquid, laying the spoon flat on the surface as you tip it, then spreading the liquid over the surface with the back of the spoon.

VARIATIONS

■ CREAM OF BROCCOLI SOUP. Prepare the soup base as described above. Meanwhile, separate the small buds and stems from 1 or 2 heads of broccoli (about 1½ pounds) and set them aside. Peel and slice the stems, and boil them over ½ inch of water (page 25). Purée them in a food processor with 1 cup of the soup base, then fold into the remaining soup. Simmer the reserved tender buds briefly in the broccoli-boiling liquid; refresh in cold water to set color; drain, and set aside; just before serving, reheat briefly in a tablespoon of butter. Rapidly boil down the cooking liquid until reduced to ½ cup, and add to the soup base. When ready to serve, heat soup to the simmer, stirring, for 2 to 3 minutes with up to ½ cup of heavy cream or sour cream. Correct seasoning and serve, decorating each portion with broccoli buds.

■ CREAM OF ASPARAGUS SOUP. Boil 2 pounds peeled fresh asparagus spears until almost tender (page 24). Refresh in cold water and cut off about 2 tender inches at the tip of each spear. Cut the bud ends off each tip, slice buds in half or quarters, and reserve for garnish— sautéing them briefly in butter before serving. Reserve the rest of the tips to purée later, and chop up the remaining stalks. Add these stalks to cook with the onions for the soup base, and purée the finished soup base through a vegetable mill to eliminate coarse asparagus strings. Purée the reserved tips (not buds!) and add to the soup base. Simmer with ½ cup or so of heavy cream or sour cream, correct seasoning, and top each portion with the sautéed asparagus buds.

■ CREAM OF CARROT SOUP. Trim and peel 8 medium-size carrots. Reserve one for garnish. Chop the rest roughly and add them to cook with the onions in the soup base. Shave reserved carrot into strips with a vegetable peeler; steam over boiling water several minutes until tender. Decorate each serving with a cluster of warm carrot strips.

■ OTHER VARIATIONS. Adapt other vegetables such as spinach, parsnips, celery, broccoli to the same system, and see also the next section using a rice purée.

FAT-FREE CREAM SOUPS WITH PURÉED RICE

You can follow this system with any of the preceding cream soups: rather than using a butter-and-flour roux for thickening, you simmer rice in the soup base until very tender. When it is turned into a very fine purée in the electric blender, you have a deliciously creamy, literally fat-free cream soup.

MASTER RECIPE

Rutabaga Soup Soubise—with Rice and Onion Purée *For about 2¼ quarts, serving 8*

¾ cup sliced celery stalks
1½ cups sliced onions

2 cups light chicken stock (page 4)
⅓ cup raw white rice
4 cups additional liquid—light chicken stock and milk
1½ quarts (2½ pounds) peeled and roughly sliced rutabaga
Salt and freshly ground white pepper
Optional: sour cream or *crème fraîche* (see box, page 9), and chopped parsley

The Rice and Onion Soup Base. Simmer the celery and onions in the 2 cups of chicken stock until very tender and translucent—15 minutes or more. Stir in the rice, and the rest of the liquid.

The Rutabaga, and Finishing the Soup. Stir in the rutabaga, bring to the simmer, season lightly, and simmer loosely covered for about 30 minutes, or until both rutabaga and rice are very tender. Purée in batches in the electric blender. Reheat, correct seasoning, and top each serving, if you wish, with a spoonful of sour cream or *crème fraîche,* and a sprinkling of chopped parsley.

VARIATIONS

■ CREAM OF CUCUMBER SOUP. For about 2¼ quarts, serving 6 to 8. Peel 4 large cucumbers, save half of one for garnish, halve the rest lengthwise, and scoop out seeds with a spoon. Chop the halves roughly and toss with 2 teaspoons each of wine vinegar and salt; let stand while the celery and onions have their preliminary simmer. Then turn the chopped cucumbers and their liquid into the soup base with the rice, and finish the soup as described in the preceding recipe. To serve, garnish with a dollop of cream, cucumber slices, and a sprinkling of fresh dill weed.

■ CREAM OF CHICKEN SOUP WITH VEGETABLES. Combine the rice-and-onion soup base with the chicken-and-vegetable soup on page 6, using only 4 cups of the liquid called for in the chicken recipe.

CHOWDERS

Traditional chowders all start off with a hearty soup base of onions and potatoes, and that makes a good soup just by itself. To this fragrant base you then add chunks of fish, or clams, or corn, or whatever else seems appropriate. (Note: You may leave out the pork and substitute another tablespoon of butter for sautéing the onions.)

The Chowder Soup Base *For about 2 quarts, to make a 2½-quart chowder serving 6 to 8*

4 ounces (⅔ cup) diced blanched salt pork or bacon (see box, page 60)
1 Tbs butter
3 cups (1 pound) sliced onions
1 imported bay leaf
¾ cup crumbled "common" or pilot crackers, or 1 pressed-down cup fresh white bread crumbs (see box, page 46)

6 cups liquid (milk, chicken stock [page
4], fish stock [page 5], clam juices, or
a combination)
3½ cups (1 pound) peeled and sliced or
diced boiling potatoes
Salt and freshly ground white pepper

Sauté the pork or bacon bits slowly
with the butter in a large saucepan for 5
minutes, or until pieces begin to brown.
Stir in the onions and bay leaf; cover,
and cook slowly 8 to 10 minutes, until
the onions are tender. Drain off fat and
blend crackers or bread crumbs into
onions. Pour in the liquid; add the potatoes and simmer, loosely covered, for
20 minutes or so, until the potatoes are
tender. Season to taste with salt and
white pepper, and the soup base is ready.

CHOWDER SUGGESTIONS

▌ NEW ENGLAND CLAM CHOWDER.
For about 2½ quarts, serving 6 to 8.
Scrub and soak 24 medium-size hard-
shell clams (see box). Steam them for 3
to 4 minutes in a large tightly covered
saucepan with 1 cup water, until most
have opened. Remove the opened clams;
cover, and steam the rest another minute
or so. Discard any unopened clams.
Pluck meat from the shells, then decant
steaming-liquid very carefully, so all
sand remains in the saucepan; include
the clam-steaming liquid as part of the
chowder base. Meanwhile, mince the
clam meats in a food processor or chop
by hand. Fold them into the finished

chowder base. Just before serving, heat
to below the simmer—so the clams
won't overcook and toughen. Fold in
a little heavy cream or sour cream if
you wish; thin with milk if necessary,
correct seasoning, and serve.

TO PREPARE CLAMS. Scrub one at a
time under running water, discarding
any that are cracked, damaged, or not
tightly closed. Soak 30 minutes in a
basin of salted water (⅓ cup salt per 4
quarts water). Lift out, and if more than
a few grains of sand remain in the basin,
repeat. Refrigerate, covered by a damp
towel. Use them within a day or two.

▌ FISH CHOWDER. Prepare the chowder
base using fish stock (page 5), and/or
light chicken stock (page 4), and milk.
Cut into 2-inch chunks 2 to 2½ pounds
of skinless, boneless lean fish, such as
cod, haddock, halibut, monkfish, or sea
bass, all one kind or a mixture. Add to
the finished chowder base and simmer 2
to 3 minutes, just until fish is opaque
and springy. Correct seasoning, and top
each serving, if you wish, with a spoonful
of sour cream.

▌ CHICKEN CHOWDER. Substitute
boneless, skinless chicken breasts for
fish, and make the chowder base with
chicken stock and milk.

▌ CORN CHOWDER. Prepare the
chowder base using 6 cups of light

chicken stock and milk. Stir 3 cups or so of grated fresh corn into the finished base, adding, if you wish, 2 green and/or red peppers chopped fine and sautéed briefly in butter. Bring to the simmer for 2 to 3 minutes; correct seasoning, and top each serving, if you wish, with a spoonful of sour cream.

TWO OF THE MOTHER SAUCES

Classical French cooking divides the sauce family into the brown sauces, the béchamel or white sauces, tomato sauce, the hollandaise or egg-yolk-and-butter sauces, the mayonnaise or egg-yolk-and-oil sauces, the vinaigrettes, and the flavored butters such as *beurre blanc*. We have brown sauces and flavored butters in the meat chapter, tomato sauces in the vegetable chapter, mayonnaise and vinaigrettes in the salad chapter, and here are béchamel and hollandaise.

MASTER RECIPE

Béchamel Sauce *For 2 cups, medium-thick*

2 Tbs unsalted butter
3 Tbs flour
2 cups hot milk
Salt and freshly ground white pepper
Pinch of nutmeg

Melt the butter in a heavy saucepan, blend in the flour with a wooden spoon, and cook over moderate heat, stirring, until butter and flour foam together for 2 minutes without turning more than a buttery yellow color. Remove from heat, and when bubbling stops, vigorously whisk in all the hot milk at once. Bring to the boil, whisking. Simmer, stirring, for 2 minutes. Season to taste.

VARIATION

▮ VELOUTÉ SAUCE. Follow the master recipe for béchamel sauce, but whisk in hot chicken or fish stock, meat juices, or vegetable broth plus milk if needed.

MASTER RECIPE

Hollandaise Sauce *For about 1½ cups*

3 egg yolks
Big pinch of salt
1 Tbs lemon juice
2 Tbs cold unsalted butter
2 sticks (8 ounces) unsalted butter, melted and hot
More salt, and freshly ground white pepper to taste

Beat the egg yolks with a wire whisk in a stainless-steel saucepan for a minute or two, until they thicken lightly and turn lemon-colored. Whisk in the pinch of salt, lemon juice, and 1 tablespoon cold butter. Set over moderately low heat and whisk continuously at moderate speed, removing pan from the heat now and then to make sure the yolks aren't cooking too fast. When they cling to the wires of the whisk and you can see the bottom of the pan between strokes, remove from heat and stir in the second tablespoon of cold butter. Start beating in the melted butter by little driblets at first, until a good ½ cup of the sauce has thickened, then add it a little more quickly as the sauce thickens into a heavy cream. Taste and correct seasoning.

TROUBLESHOOTING HOLLANDAISE SAUCE. If you have added the butter too fast for the egg yolks to digest it, or if you've kept the sauce over heat too long, it can thin out or separate. To bring it back to its creamy state, whisk it briefly to blend, and dip a tablespoonful into a bowl. Whisk in a tablespoon of lemon juice and whisk vigorously until creamy. Then whisk in very little dribbles of the turned sauce at first, not adding more until the previous addition has creamed and the sauce begins to reconstitute.

MACHINE-MADE HOLLANDAISE. The handmade sauce is easy and relatively quick when you are used to it, but you may prefer the electric blender. Use the same system, but it's so difficult to try and get most—never all—of that sticky sauce out of the blender! And then you have to reheat it. However, if it's to be a machine I prefer the food processor, and I also recommend the processor for mayonnaise.

VARIATION

■ BÉARNAISE SAUCE. For about 1 cup. Bring ¼ cup each of wine vinegar and dry white wine or dry white French vermouth to the boil in a small saucepan, adding 1 tablespoon minced shallots, ½ teaspoon dried tarragon, and ¼ teaspoon each of salt and freshly ground pepper. Boil rapidly until the liquid is reduced to 2 tablespoons; strain, if you wish, pressing liquid from seasonings. Substitute this essence for the lemon juice in the preceding master recipe but add only 1½ sticks of butter in all, to make an authoritative sauce. You may wish to stir chopped fresh tarragon leaves into the finished sauce.

Salads and Their Dressings

"The perfect vinaigrette is so easy to make that I see no reason whatsoever for bottled dressings."

Although we always have with us those hard-core purists who profess to eat fresh produce only when it is locally "in season," now, with modern packaging, state-of-the-art refrigeration, and rapid transport, we can have almost every kind of fresh produce all year round. We have not yet solved the tomato problem, but certainly greens abound in glorious variety, as do so many other desirable items that are ready and waiting to grace our salad days.

SALAD GREENS

Once you have brought your greens home you naturally want to keep them as fresh and perky as possible. If they are ready trimmed, washed, and packaged, they'll keep for several days as is. I'm most enthusiastic about the hydroponic "living lettuce," which keeps perfectly in the refrigerator for a week or more, sitting on its still-attached root in its plastic box. I don't even wash mine; I'm just careful, when I pull off the leaves, not to disturb the root.

Slightly Wilted Greens. If this happens to yours, you can often bring them back to a reasonable crispness by soaking for several hours in a basin of cold water.

To Wash Greens, such as Boston or butter lettuce, curly endive, romaine, oak leaf, escarole, and radicchio, discard wilted leaves and/or tear off wilted parts of leaves. Separate leaves from root ends and, if you wish, tear leaves off from central stems, then tear leaves into serving pieces. Plunge them into a large basin of cold water, pump up and down, let settle a moment so sand will sink to the bottom, then lift the leaves out with your hands, leaving sand behind.

To Dry Greens. Spin dry a few handfuls at a time in a salad basket.

To Keep Washed Greens. A most effective system for several hours' wait, and if you have room, is to lay them out hollow side down on paper towels in a deep roasting pan; cover with a damp towel and refrigerate. Otherwise, I pack the leaves loosely and refrigerate them surrounded by dampened paper towels in a big plastic bag, where they keep for 2 days or so.

Mixed Green Salad

A pound or so of salad greens will serve 6—all one kind, such as 1 large head of Boston lettuce, or a mixture. The greens are washed and dried, and torn into whatever size you prefer—small pieces are easier to eat, but larger ones toss more attractively and are usually more appealing on the plate. Your salad dressing has been prepared. You have a large bowl at the ready, and a long-handled salad fork and spoon. The moment before serving (and not before, or the salad will wilt), turn the greens into the bowl. Toss with several spoonfuls of the dressing, reaching down into the bottom of the bowl with your spoon and fork and bringing up big clumps of leaves, and repeating rapidly, adding driblets of dressing as needed so that all the leaves are lightly enrobed but the greens are not swimming. Pick up a small piece and taste analytically, tossing in a sprinkling of salt and pepper or more lemon or vinegar if needed. Serve at once.

SALAD DRESSINGS

The perfect dressing is essential to the perfect salad, and I see no reason whatsoever for using a bottled dressing, which may have been sitting on the grocery shelf for weeks, even months—even years. With your own dressing everything is fresh—the best oil, your own choice of vinegar, fresh lemon—and a really good salad dressing is so quick and easy to make, as described here.

SALAD OILS AND VINEGARS. The choice is entirely up to you, the main consideration being taste. You may sometimes prefer a fruity olive oil over a mild one, or you may like peanut or vegetable oil for certain dishes—just make certain it is fresh and fine. The same goes for vinegar, and be sure you know the taste of a wine vinegar before you buy it, since there is quite a variety in qualities. I personally have always bought the French vinegar from Orléans, because I am used to it, but I have tasted some excellent domestic ones. When you have been served a salad with a particularly fine dressing, ask your hosts how they did it—they'll be complimented and you'll be adding a new page to your kitchen recipe files.

Basic Vinaigrette Dressing

This is a bare-bones recipe for the simple all-purpose vinaigrette, which you will vary as you wish; you'll find suggestions at the end of this recipe. Its beauty lies solely in the quality of your ingredients. Note that you will so often see proportions of 1 part vinegar to 3 parts oil, but that can make a very acid, very vinegary vinaigrette. I use the proportions of a very dry martini, since you can always add more vinegar or lemon but you can't take it out.

For about ⅔ cup, serving 6 to 8

½ Tbs finely minced shallot or scallion
½ Tbs Dijon-type mustard
¼ tsp salt
½ Tbs freshly squeezed lemon juice
½ Tbs wine vinegar
⅓ to ½ cup excellent olive oil, or other fine, fresh oil
Freshly ground pepper

Either shake all the ingredients together in a screw-topped jar, or mix them individually as follows. Stir the shallots or scallions together with the mustard and salt. Whisk in the lemon juice and vinegar, and when well blended start whisking in the oil by droplets to form a smooth emulsion. Beat in freshly ground pepper. Taste (dip a piece of the salad greens into the sauce) and correct seasoning with salt, pepper, and/or drops of lemon juice.

TO KEEP SALAD DRESSING. Vinaigrette is always at its freshest and best when served promptly, but you can certainly cover it airtight and refrigerate it for several days. The shallots and fresh lemon will eventually go off, spoiling the taste of the dressing.

VARIATIONS

▌ GARLIC. Purée the garlic (see box, page 34) and add it to or substitute it for the minced shallots. Or rub the salad bowl with a peeled clove of garlic. Or rub a peeled clove of garlic over dry-toasted French-bread rounds (see box, page 7), cut into pieces, and toss with the salad.

▌ LEMON PEEL. For a pronounced lemon flavor, mince the zest (colored part of peel only) of a shiny fresh lemon and stir it into the sauce.

▌ HERBS. Mince fresh herbs such as parsley, chives, chervil, tarragon, basil, and/or dill and whisk into the finished dressing.

▌ SWEET AND SOUR DRESSING. Especially for duck, goose, pork, game. Beat a tablespoon of hoisin sauce or minced chutney into the vinaigrette, including, if you wish, droplets of dark sesame oil. (See page 18 on using this dressing in a duck salad.)

▌ ROQUEFORT DRESSING. Crumble about ⅓ cup of Roquefort cheese and stir into the ⅔ cup of vinaigrette—or use whatever proportions you wish. A particular favorite of mine, served at the Café de Sevilla in Santa Barbara, is to halve or quarter romaine hearts, set them cut side up on serving dishes, and spoon over them the Roquefort dressing.

Chopped Hard-Boiled Eggs—Salad Mimosa

For 6 servings. Neatly dice 2 hard-boiled eggs and toss with 2 tablespoons of minced herbs such as parsley, chives, basil, and/or tarragon. Season lightly with salt and pepper, and sprinkle over the dressed salad just before serving.

Curly Endive with Bacon and Poached Eggs

For 6 servings. Poach 6 eggs (page 67). Cut a 2-inch square of slab bacon into *lardons* (see box, page 60), brown lightly in a frying pan, and drain, leaving ½ tablespoon bacon fat in the pan. Make your vinaigrette right in the frying pan, including the bacon fat as part of the dressing. Toss the curly endive with the dressing, and top each serving with the bacon *lardons* and a poached egg. Garnish with a sprinkling of chopped parsley.

Warm Duck Leg Salad

Particularly recommended when you have used the breast of a roaster duckling, and have uncooked legs to spare. Bone them, skin them, and pound meat between sheets of plastic wrap to a thickness of ¼ inch, then cut into strips ¼ inch wide. Stir-fry briefly in a little olive oil until lightly browned but still rosy inside. Toss with the sweet and sour dressing, and serve on a bed of frizzy lettuce.

MAIN COURSE SALADS

Salade Niçoise

Of all main-course salads, the Niçoise is my all-time favorite, with its fresh butter-lettuce foundation; its carefully cooked, beautifully green green beans; its colorful contrast of halved hard-boiled eggs, ripe red tomatoes, and black olives; all fortified by chunks of tunafish and freshly opened anchovies (see box, page 19). It's a perfect luncheon dish, to my mind, winter, summer, spring, and fall—an inspired combination that pleases everyone.

Serves 6

1 large head Boston-lettuce leaves, washed and dried
1 pound green beans, cooked and refreshed (page 25)
1½ Tbs minced shallots
½ to ⅔ cup basic vinaigrette (page 16)
Salt and freshly ground pepper
3 or 4 ripe red tomatoes, cut into wedges (or 10 to 12 cherry tomatoes, halved)

3 or 4 "boiling" potatoes, peeled, sliced, and cooked (see potato salad, page 20)

Two 3-ounce cans chunk tuna, preferably oil-packed

6 hard-boiled eggs, peeled and halved (page 70)

1 freshly opened can of flat anchovy fillets (see box)

⅓ cup small black Niçoise-type olives

2 to 3 Tbs capers

3 Tbs minced fresh parsley

Arrange the lettuce leaves on a large platter or in a shallow bowl. Shortly before serving, toss the beans with the shallots, spoonfuls of vinaigrette, and salt and pepper. Baste the tomatoes with a spoonful of vinaigrette. Place the potatoes in the center of the platter and arrange a mound of beans at either end, with tomatoes and small mounds of tuna at strategic intervals. Ring the platter with halves of hard-boiled eggs, sunny side up, and curl an anchovy on top of each. Spoon more vinaigrette over all; scatter on olives, capers, and parsley, and serve.

VARIATIONS

■ COLD ROAST MEAT SALAD. Thinly slice, or cut into cubes or strips, a pound of cold roast or braised beef, veal, or pork, and refrigerate for several hours in a bowl with sufficient vinaigrette to enrobe the pieces, turning and basting several times. To serve, arrange nicely on a platter, surrounded with pickles, capers, olives, tomatoes, sliced red onions and green peppers, cooked green beans, or whatever appeals to you.

FRESHLY OPENED CAN OF ANCHOVIES. Anchovies go "off" in taste when they sit around in an open can—which is probably why many people hate anchovies.

■ SYRIAN LAMB SALAD. Marinate for several hours a dozen thin slices of cold roast leg of lamb in garlic-flavored vinaigrette plus several puréed freshly opened anchovies. Mound 3 cups or so of prepared bulgur (cracked wheat; see box) in the center of a platter, and surround with the lamb slices. Garnish as you wish with olives, hard-boiled eggs, tomato wedges, sliced bell peppers, marinated cucumber (page 23).

TO PREPARE BULGUR—CRACKED WHEAT. Stir a quart of boiling water into 1 cup raw, dry bulgur. Let sit 15 minutes, or until pleasantly tender. Drain, rinse in cold water, and squeeze dry in a towel. Toss with 1 Tbs each of olive oil, grated onion, and chopped parsley. Season to taste with salt, pepper, and lemon juice.

■ BREAST OF PHEASANT, DUCK, CHICKEN, OR TURKEY SERVED IN A SALAD. Marinate slices of the cooked breast for 30 minutes or so in the vinaigrette. Then, for each serving, arrange several strips over a bed of tender frizzy lettuce leaves. Baste with vinaigrette and decorate with small segments of orange, thin red-onion slices, and a spoonful of toasted pine nuts.

MASTER RECIPE

Chicken Salad *Serves 6 to 8*

6 cups cooked chicken, cut up into good-
    sized pieces
Salt and freshly ground white pepper
1 to 2 Tbs olive oil
2 to 3 Tbs fresh lemon juice
1 cup diced tender celery stalks
½ cup diced red onion
1 cup chopped walnuts
½ cup chopped parsley
1 tsp finely cut fresh tarragon leaves
    (or ¼ tsp dried tarragon)
⅔ cup or so mayonnaise
    (see box, page 21)
Fresh salad greens, washed and dried
For decoration: all or a choice of sliced
    or chopped hard-boiled eggs, parsley
    sprigs, strips of red pimiento

Toss the chicken with salt, pepper, olive oil, lemon juice, celery, onion, and walnuts. Cover and refrigerate at least 20 minutes or overnight. Drain out any accumulated liquid; toss with the parsley and tarragon. Taste analytically and correct seasonings. Fold in just enough mayonnaise to enrobe ingredients. Shred the greens, arrange on a platter, and mound the salad on top. Spread a thin coat of mayonnaise over the chicken and decorate with the eggs, parsley, and pimiento strips.

VARIATIONS

▮ TURKEY SALAD. Follow the same general system as for chicken.

▮ LOBSTER, CRAB, OR SHRIMP SALAD. Follow the same general system, and use some of the shells for decoration.

Pasta Salad

On one of our television shoots we had a caterer who started us out with a quite acceptable pasta salad but then let it continue, recycled and recycled, day after day, for a week; finally, rebellion forced a change of caterers. I've never much cared for the dish since, but I do admit it can be good when creatively made. I even showed a children's version myself on the TV show *Mister Rogers' Neighborhood.* It was regular long spaghetti cooked, drained, and tossed with olive oil, salt and pepper, diced green and red peppers, scallions, black olives, and walnut meats. "Spaghetti Marco Polo." We ate it with chopsticks.

American-Style Potato Salad

The Potato Base. Halve 3 pounds of "boiling" potatoes and slice 3/16 inch thick. Boil in lightly salted water for 3 to 5 minutes, just until tender. Drain out cooking water, then cover the pan and let sit 3 to 4 minutes, to firm up. In a large mixing bowl, gently fold the slices with salt, pepper, ½ cup minced onions, and

¾ cup chicken broth; let sit for a few minutes, then very gently fold and let sit twice more.

The Finish. Fold in a finely chopped dill pickle, 3 or 4 chopped hard-boiled eggs, 3 or 4 finely diced tender celery ribs, and 4 or 5 strips of crumbled crisp bacon. Let salad cool, then fold in enough mayonnaise just to enrobe the potatoes. Correct seasoning, and garnish if you wish with hard-boiled eggs and parsley.

VARIATIONS

▮ FRENCH POTATO SALAD. Prepare the potato base as described, and, while still warm, fold in olive oil, chopped parsley, and seasonings to taste. Let cool.

▮ WARM POTATO SALAD WITH SAUSAGES. Prepare the French potato salad above, and serve warm with generous slices of delicious warm sausage.

PROCESSOR MAYONNAISE. Break 1 whole egg into the container of a food processor, add 2 egg yolks, and process 30 to 45 seconds, or until thick and lemon-colored. With the machine running, add 1 tablespoon fresh lemon juice and/or wine vinegar, 1 teaspoon Dijon-type mustard, ½ teaspoon salt, and several grinds of white pepper. Still with the machine running, and by very small dribbles at first, start adding up to 2 cups of olive oil and/or vegetable oil. After about ½ cup has gone in, add the oil a little faster, until you have a thick mayonnaise. Taste carefully, processing in lemon or vinegar and seasonings as needed.

Storage. Refrigerate in a covered container; the sauce will keep for about a week. Note that a chilled sauce can sometimes turn or thin out when stirred up—best to transfer it by spoonfuls into a warmed mixing bowl, whisking as you add each to the bowl.

Troubleshooting. If the sauce separates or thins out, let it sit for several minutes, until the oil has risen over the clotted residue. Spoon as much of the oil as you quite easily can into a separate bowl. Dip a tablespoon of the residue into a clean bowl. By hand or with a portable mixer, whisk it vigorously with ½ tablespoon of Dijon-type mustard until creamed and thickened. Then by half teaspoons at first, whisk in additional residue, letting the sauce cream and thicken after each addition. Finally, continue with the oil, adding it by dribbles. (Note that using the same techniques you can also accomplish this in the electric blender.)

COLE SLAW AND OTHER VEGETABLE SALADS

Cole Slaw *Serves 6 to 8*

1½ pounds firm fresh cabbage,
    finely shredded (see box)
½ cup grated carrots
⅔ cup diced tender celery stalks
1 medium cucumber, peeled, halved
    lengthwise, seeded, and diced
½ cup finely diced green bell pepper
¼ cup finely diced yellow onion
1 small tart apple, peeled, cored, and
    finely diced
¼ cup chopped fresh parsley

For Dressing the Slaw

1 Tbs Dijon-type mustard
3 Tbs cider vinegar
1 tsp salt
1 tsp sugar
¼ tsp caraway or cumin seeds
¼ tsp celery seeds
Freshly ground pepper
½ cup or so mayonnaise, optional
⅓ cup sour cream, optional

Toss the cabbage in a large mixing bowl with the other vegetables, apple, and parsley. Mix the mustard, vinegar, salt, and sugar together, pour into the bowl, and toss with the cabbage. Fold in the caraway or cumin, celery seed, and pepper. Taste and adjust seasoning. Let stand for 30 minutes, or cover and refrigerate. Before serving, drain out accumulated liquid and adjust seasoning again. Serve as is, or blend mayonnaise and sour cream together and fold into the slaw.

MACHINE-SHREDDED CABBAGE. Slice off the top and the bottom of the cabbage. Halve the head and cut out the central core. Cut the halves into wedges that will fit into your food processor, cut sides down. Using the slicing disk, process wedge by wedge to produce finely shredded cabbage.

Celery Root Rémoulade

Working quickly to prevent discoloration, peel a 1-pound head of celeriac, cut into chunks, and shred in a food processor or hand-held vegetable-julienne machine. At once, toss with ½ teaspoon of salt and 1½ tablespoons of lemon juice and let macerate 30 minutes. For the dressing, whisk ¼ cup Dijon-type mustard in a warm mixing bowl, dribbling in 3 tablespoons boiling water followed, in dribbles, by ⅓ cup olive oil or vegetable oil and 2 tablespoons wine vinegar, to make a thick, creamy sauce. Fold into the celery root, correct seasoning, and garnish with chopped parsley. You may serve at once, or cover and let steep for an hour or longer in the refrigerator, where it will improve in flavor and tenderness.

Grated Beet Salad

For 2 pounds of beets, serving 6. Peel the beets and put through the large holes of a hand grater or a processor. Sauté briefly in 2 tablespoons olive oil and a large clove of puréed garlic just to heat through, tossing to blend with salt, pepper, and 1 tablespoon wine vinegar. Stir in ¼ cup water, cover, and boil slowly for 10 minutes or until beets are tender and water has evaporated. Let cool and toss with more oil, vinegar, and seasonings to taste. Serve with salad greens, or spears of Belgian endive.

VARIATION

■ SLICED BEET SALAD. Using whole peeled warm beets (see box), slice them and toss in a bowl with olive oil, puréed garlic (see box, page 34), and salt to taste.

BEETS IN THE PRESSURE COOKER. Whole beets take hours to cook in the oven but only 20 minutes in the pressure cooker. Place 2-inch washed unpeeled beets on the rack in the cooker with 1 inch of water. Bring to full 15 pounds pressure and time for 20 minutes. Set under the cold-water faucet to release pressure immediately. Peel the beets while still warm.

Cucumber Salad

For 6 servings, or as a garnish. Peel, halve lengthwise, and scoop the seeds out of 2 large cucumbers. Cut either into thin slices or into julienne, and toss with ½ teaspoon salt, ¼ teaspoon sugar, and 1 teaspoon wine vinegar. Let steep for 15 to 20 minutes, then drain (you may wish to save the liquid for salad dressing). Serve as is, tossed with chopped parsley or fresh dill, or fold with sour cream and then garnish with dill.

NOTE: Most store-bought cucumbers are coated in wax, as a preservative. If yours are uncoated, no need to peel them, and you will have the pleasure of green-bordered cucumber slices. Coated or not, no need to seed them, although if unseeded they will exude more liquid when dressed.

Vegetables

"When you serve fine, fresh green vegetables, you want them to show off their color."

Little white onions must hold their shape but be tender all the way through, and your mashed potatoes are to be smooth and full of that good potato flavor. Here are my suggestions as to whether you will achieve the best results by steaming them, boiling them, or cover-cooking them in a braise.

THE BLANCH/BOIL SYSTEM FOR GREEN VEGETABLES

To blanch/boil a green vegetable, like green beans, you plunge them into a large pot of rapidly boiling water, bring back to the boil as fast as possible, and boil slowly for a few minutes, until the vegetable is just tender. The large amount of water—6 to 8 quarts for 2 pounds of beans, for instance—means that it will come quickly back to the boil, thus setting the color. If you are not serving them almost at once, drain immediately and run cold water into the kettle, again to preserve the color, and also the texture. Drain thoroughly, and the vegetables are ready to serve either hot or cold. Thus you can cook them several hours in advance. Note that salt proportions are 1½ teaspoons salt per quart of water, making 12 teaspoons (4 tablespoons or ¼ cup) for 8 quarts.

BLANCH/BOIL VEGETABLE CHART

Vegetable	Preparation	Cooking (In 6 to 8 quarts of salted water at a rapid boil)	Finishing
Asparagus (4 to 6 spears per serving)	Trim ½ inch off tough ends and peel spears from butt to just below tip.	Lay flat and boil uncovered 4 to 5 minutes, or until asparagus bends slightly. Remove and drain on a towel.	Drizzle melted butter and/or fresh lemon juice over warm asparagus. Or serve with hollandaise (page 13). Or serve cold with vinaigrette (page 16).

Vegetable	Preparation	Cooking (In 6 to 8 quarts of salted water at a rapid boil)	Finishing
Broccoli (1½ lbs, to serve 4 or 5)	Cut off florets and peel stems. Peel central stalks to pale interior and cut in pieces.	Boil uncovered 2 to 4 minutes, until tender with only a slight crunch remaining. Remove immediately. Broccoli cooks (and overcooks) so quickly I don't recommend it be done in advance.	Same suggestions as for asparagus plus: 1- Sprinkle on fresh bread crumbs (see box, page 46), sautéed in butter. 2- Toss the broccoli in a sauté pan with olive oil and puréed garlic. 3- Prepare au gratin (page 31).
Brussels Sprouts (1½ lbs, to serve 4 or 5)	Trim root ends, remove loose or discolored leaves; pierce a cross ¼ inch deep in root ends.	Boil uncovered 4 to 5 minutes, until just tender when pierced. Drain. Refresh in cold water if not served at once.	1- Serve whole with melted butter, or cut in half and sauté in hot butter until slightly browned. 2- Prepare au gratin (page 31).
Green Beans (1½ lbs, to serve 4 or 5)	For thin beans and *haricots verts,* snap off ends. For wide beans, "french" them by slicing diagonally into 1-inch strips.	Cook "frenched" beans 2 to 3 minutes, or whole beans 4 to 5 minutes, until just cooked through. Drain immediately; finish immediately or refresh under cold water.	1- Toss in a frying pan with butter, lemon juice, seasonings, and parsley. 2- Chill and toss with vinaigrette (page 16).
Spinach (3 lbs, to serve 4)	Rinse in cold water, lift out, and repeat to remove sand. Pull stems from leaves.	Boil uncovered until limp, 1 to 3 minutes, depending on maturity. Drain; refresh under cold water; drain; squeeze dry and chop by hand. (If young and tender, no need to boil, simply sauté in oil or butter.)	Sauté briefly in butter or olive oil, with minced garlic. Or sauté, then add ½ to 1 cup stock or cream, and season with salt, pepper, and nutmeg. Cover and braise 5 to 7 minutes in butter and shallots, until tender.

Vegetable	Preparation	Cooking (In 6 to 8 quarts of salted water at a rapid boil)	Finishing
Swiss Chard (10 stalks, to serve 6 to 8)	Cut leaves from central white stalk. Cook leaves and stalks separately.	The stalk: Cut into ¼-inch slices. Whisk 3 cups water gradually into ¼ cup flour with 1 tsp salt and 1 Tbs lemon juice. Bring to boil, add stalks, and simmer 30 minutes. Drain. The leaves: Boil, squeeze dry, and chop, as for spinach.	Prepare the leaves in any of the ways suggested for spinach. Or toss leaves and stalks together and bake them with cheese au gratin, as for the cauliflower (page 31), using the stalk-cooking liquid as your sauce base.

STEAMED VEGETABLES

When you are not concerned with preserving the color, steaming is an easy way to cook a number of vegetables. You will want a vegetable-steamer basket that fits into a pan with a tight-fitting cover. Pour 1 inch of water into the pan, set the steamer basket in the pan, and arrange the vegetables in the basket. Cover, bring to the boil, and start timing as soon as the steam rises.

A HANDFUL OF STEAMED VEGETABLES

Vegetable	Preparation	Cooking (In basket over 1 inch liquid, in covered pot)	Finishing
Artichokes (whole, 1 per person)	Trim stem off base. Cut ½ inch off top; snip prickly points off leaves with scissors. Rub cut parts with lemon.	Arrange upside down in basket. Steam over water 30 to 40 minutes, until bottoms are tender when pierced.	1- Serve warm with melted butter or hollandaise (page 13) for dipping leaves. 2- Serve cold with mayonnaise (page 21), or vinaigrette (page 16).

Vegetable	Preparation	Cooking (In 6 to 8 quarts of salted water at a rapid boil)	Finishing
Cabbage Wedges (a 2-lb. cabbage serves 4)	Cut cabbage in half through the core; cut halves into wedges. Trim core but don't let leaves separate.	Arrange cabbage wedges cut sides up on steamer rack. Pour over them 2 cups chicken stock plus water to a depth of 1 inch in the pan. Season wedges, cover pot, and steam about 15 minutes, until just tender.	Rapidly boil down steaming liquid until syrupy. Swirl in 1 to 2 Tbs butter and chopped parsley. Drizzle over the cabbage for serving.
Cauliflower (1½ lbs, to serve 4 or 5)	Cut out central core and break florets apart. Peel core deeply and cut into pieces. Peel stems of florets.	Steam over water 3 to 5 minutes, until cooked through but with slight crunch.	1- Top with butter, lemon, or hollandaise; or sprinkle on sautéed buttered bread crumbs and chopped parsley. 2- Toss pieces in a frying pan with olive oil, puréed garlic, and parsley. 3- Prepare gratin (page 31).
Eggplant (a 1-lb. eggplant serves 4)	Wash eggplant. Place whole in basket.	Steam over water 20 to 30 minutes, until soft, slightly shriveled, and easily pierced.	Trim off green cap and slice eggplant in halves or quarters lengthwise. 1- Drizzle flesh with garlicky vinaigrette (page 17) serve warm or cool. 2- Scoop out flesh; sauté slowly in olive oil with onions and puréed garlic, until tender and slightly browned. 3- Eggplant caviar: Purée flesh in a mixer, then beat in puréed garlic, allspice, ginger, Tabasco, and, if you wish, a cup of ground walnuts, plus up to 4 Tbs olive oil added by drops.

THE BOIL/STEAM SYSTEM FOR VEGETABLES

This is an especially effective method for root vegetables such as carrots and small onions, as well as for store-bought green peas. Rather than boiling the vegetables in water to cover, then draining them, thus throwing out a lot of the flavor with the cooking liquid, you want to cover-cook them in a small amount of liquid. You then boil down that liquid to concentrate its flavor, and use it to sauce your vegetables.

BOIL/STEAM VEGETABLE CHART

Vegetable	Preparation	Cooking	Finishing
Green Peas (2 lbs fresh store-bought peas in the pod, making about 3 cups, to serve 6)	Shell peas into a saucepan. Add 1 Tbs of soft butter, and ½ tsp each salt and sugar. By handfuls, bruise the peas roughly with the butter, sugar, and salt.	Pour in water almost to cover peas. Bring to boil, cover, and cook at the rapid boil 10 to 15 minutes, or until tender.	Uncover and boil off liquid if necessary. Correct seasoning. Toss with more butter if you wish.
Small White Onions (12 to 16 onions, about 1 inch diameter, to serve 4)	To peel, drop onions into boiling water for exactly 1 minute. Drain and refresh in cold water. Shave off ends; slip off skins. Pierce a cross ¼ inch deep in root ends, to prevent bursting.	For "white-braised" onions: Arrange in 1 layer in a saucepan with chicken stock or water to come halfway up. Add 1 Tbs butter, season lightly, cover, and simmer slowly 25 minutes, or until tender. For "brown-braised" onions: Before steaming, sauté peeled onions in 1 layer in butter and oil until colored. Then add liquid, salt, and 1 tsp sugar; cover and cook as above.	1- Uncover, boil off excess liquid, and fold in another Tbs of butter if you wish. 2- For creamed onions: Add heavy cream to white-braised onions when they are just tender. Simmer several minutes until thickened, basting. Fold in chopped parsley if you wish.

Vegetable	Preparation	Cooking	Finishing
Carrots, Parsnips, Rutabagas, Turnips (1½ lbs, to serve 5 or 6)	Peel the vegetables and cut into ¾-inch chunks.	Place in saucepan; add water to come halfway up the vegetables. Season with ½ tsp salt and, if you wish, 1 or 2 Tbs butter. Cover and boil hard over high heat 8 to 10 minutes, or until tender. Uncover and rapidly boil down liquid until evaporated.	1- Toss chunks with butter and chopped parsley and/or scallions, or with grated fresh ginger. 2- Purée steamed chunks in food mill or processor. Stir over moderate heat in a heavy pan to evaporate moisture. Stir in butter or heavy cream; season to taste. 3- Golden purée: Blend puréed carrots (or squash) with mashed potatoes (page 34).
Winter Squash (1½ lbs squash, to serve 5 or 6)	Cut in half and scrape out seeds and strings. Peel halves and cut into ¾-inch chunks	Cook as described above.	Purée as described above.

ROASTED OR BAKED VEGETABLES

Although they are synonymous, "roasted" sounds more exciting to the modern ear than "baked," which has a rather dowdy and old-fashioned ring. I shall use whichever sounds best to me.

Tomatoes Provençal

Halved and baked with herbs, garlic, and crumbs. For 4 firm, ripe tomatoes, to serve 4. Halve, seed, and juice the tomatoes (see box, page 30). Toss together ½ cup fresh white bread crumbs, 2 tablespoons minced shallots or scallions, 2 cloves garlic, minced, 1 to 2 Tbs olive oil, and salt and pepper to taste. Salt lightly, and fill tomatoes with the crumb mixture.

Drizzle on olive oil and bake in the upper level of a preheated 400°F oven for 15 to 20 minutes, until crumbs are lightly browned and tomatoes are softened but still hold their shape.

TOMATOES: PEELED, SEEDED, AND JUICED—FRESH TOMATO PULP. To peel tomatoes, drop them into a large pan of rapidly boiling water and time the boil for exactly 10 seconds. Cut out the core, then peel the skin down from it. To seed and juice them, halve crosswise and gently squeeze to dislodge jelly and juice, poking out remaining seeds with your fingers. They are then usually chopped or diced (*concassées*) into "fresh tomato pulp."

Baked Winter Squash

For 1½ pounds squash, to serve 4 to 6. To bake any winter squash, halve it and scrape out seeds and strings. Rub the inside with butter and seasonings, then bake in the lower-third level of a preheated 400°F oven until the flesh is soft and edible, usually an hour or more. Cut into serving portions and serve as is, or fill with any stuffing suitable for turkey and bake another ½ hour, basting several times with roasting juices or melted butter.

Baked Eggplant Slices and Eggplant "Pizza"

For 2 medium eggplants, about 3 pounds, to serve 5 or 6. Choose firm, shiny eggplants. Wash them and cut into ½-inch slices, salt lightly on both sides, and let sweat on paper towels 20 to 30 minutes. Pat dry, arrange on an oiled baking pan, and brush tops with olive oil. Sprinkle on dried Italian or Provençal herbs (see box, page 44), cover with foil, and bake in a preheated 400°F oven for 20 minutes, or until just tender. For eggplant "pizza," spread tomato sauce (see box) over each slice, and sprinkle with Parmesan and a drizzle of olive oil. Brown under the broiler.

TOMATO SAUCE

FRESH TOMATO SAUCE. For about 2½ cups, sauté ½ cup minced onions in 2 tablespoons olive oil, and when tender stir in 4 cups fresh tomato pulp (see box, left) or half fresh and half canned Italian plum tomatoes. Season with a pinch of thyme, a bay leaf, 2 large cloves of puréed garlic, and, if you wish, both a pinch of saffron threads and ¼ teaspoon dried orange peel. Salt lightly and simmer, partially covered, for 30 minutes.

TOMATO FONDUE—A GARNISH. Sauté 2 tablespoons minced shallots or scallions in 1 tablespoon olive oil or butter, and when tender bring to the boil with ¼ cup each of chicken stock and dry white French vermouth. When syrupy, blend in 2 cups fresh tomato pulp (see box above), a clove of minced garlic, and a good pinch of tarragon or basil. Simmer 2 to 3 minutes to cook the tomatoes, then correct seasoning and fold in minced parsley.

Cauliflower au Gratin

To serve 5 or 6. For 3 cups of cooked cauliflower (see charts), prepare 2 to 2½ cups béchamel sauce (page 13). Fold ⅓ cup of coarsely grated Swiss cheese into the sauce, and spread a thin layer in a buttered shallow baking dish. Arrange the cauliflower in the dish, spoon over the remaining sauce, and sprinkle on ¼ cup of cheese. Bake in a preheated 425°F oven 20 to 25 minutes, until bubbling and lightly browned on top.

VARIATIONS

▮ BROCCOLI OR BRUSSELS SPROUTS. Use exactly the same system as for cauliflower.

▮ ZUCCHINI AU GRATIN. Grate and sauté zucchini (page 32) but save the squeezed-out zucchini juices. Make a velouté sauce (page 13), using 2 tablespoons butter, 3 tablespoons flour, and 1½ cups liquid (zucchini juices plus milk). Fold the zucchini into the sauce, spread in a buttered baking dish, and sprinkle over ¼ cup grated Swiss cheese. Bake in upper-third level of a 400°F oven until bubbling and browned, about 20 minutes.

SAUTÉED VEGETABLES

As always, sautéing is the easiest and fastest way to prepare vegetables. However, you always have to remember the added calories given you by that delicious butter or virgin olive oil you are using.

Sautéed Mushrooms

Keep in mind: 1 pound fresh mushrooms = 1 quart; ½ pound sliced fresh mushrooms = 2½ cups; ½ pound diced fresh mushrooms = 2 cups; ¾ pound (3 cups) sliced or quartered fresh mushrooms = 2 cups sautéed mushrooms.

For ¾ pound quartered fresh mushrooms, heat 1½ tablespoons butter and ½ tablespoon oil in a large frying pan,

and when butter foam is subsiding, turn in the mushrooms. Sauté for several minutes, tossing frequently as the butter is absorbed and then reappears on the surface when the mushrooms begin to brown. Toss in ½ tablespoon chopped shallots, season with salt and pepper, and sauté another 30 seconds.

■ MUSHROOM DUXELLES—FINELY DICED SAUTÉED MUSHROOMS. Finely dice ½ quart (½ pound) fresh mushrooms. By handfuls, twist them in the corner of a towel to extract their juices. Sauté as previously directed, adding chopped shallots at the end. For a wine flavoring, stir in 2 tablespoons dry port or Madeira and boil down briefly.

SIMMERED MUSHROOM CAPS. For use as a garnish. Toss 10 large mushroom caps in a stainless-steel saucepan with ¼ cup water, 1 tablespoon fresh lemon juice, a big pinch of salt, and 1 tablespoon butter. Simmer, covered, for 2 to 3 minutes until just tender.

Pipérade—Sautéed Peppers and Onions

For 1½ cups. Sauté 1 sliced medium onion slowly in 2 tablespoons olive oil until tender but not browned. Add 1 sliced medium red pepper, 1 sliced green pepper, and a clove of puréed garlic. Season with a big pinch of Provençal herbs (see box, page 44), and salt and pepper to taste. Continue sautéing several minutes over low heat, until peppers are tender.

Grated Sautéed Zucchini

For 1½ pounds, to serve 4. Grate the zucchini and toss in a colander with 1½

teaspoons salt; let steep 20 minutes. By handfuls, twist in the corner of a towel to extract juices. Sauté 1 tablespoon minced shallot briefly in a large frying pan with 2 tablespoons olive oil or butter, then add the zucchini and toss over high heat for 2 minutes or so, just until tender.

■ CREAMED ZUCCHINI. When tender, stir in ½ cup of heavy cream and let simmer until absorbed, then fold with a tablespoon of chopped parsley or tarragon.

■ GRATINÉED WITH CHEESE. See page 31.

Grated Sautéed/Steamed Beets

For 1½ pounds beets, to serve 4. Peel and grate the beets. Toss them in a nonstick frying pan with 2 tablespoons melted butter. Add ¼ inch water and 1 teaspoon red-wine vinegar, and bring to simmer over medium heat for 1 minute, stirring. Cover, lower heat, and simmer about 10 minutes, adding more water if necessary, until beets are tender and liquid has evaporated. Swirl and toss with another tablespoon or so of butter, and season to taste.

■ TURNIPS, RUTABAGAS, AND CARROTS. Grate and sauté/steam the same way.

Brown Onion "Marmalade"

To make about ½ cup. Sauté 3 cups sliced onions slowly in 2 to 3 tablespoons butter for about 15 minutes, until tender and translucent. Raise heat and sauté 5 minutes or so more, stirring, until nicely browned.

BRAISED VEGETABLES

When vegetables need longer cooking, you braise them, meaning you cover them and let them steam in their own juices.

Braised Celery

Use ⅓ to ½ prepared celery heart per serving. Cut the celery hearts in halves or thirds lengthwise, depending on thickness; wash under cold running water. Lay cut side up in a buttered flameproof baking dish. Salt lightly, spread over each a teaspoon of mirepoix (see box), and pour in chicken stock to a third of the way up. Bring to the simmer on top of the stove. Lay buttered wax paper over the celery, cover with foil, and cook in a 350°F oven 30 to 40 minutes, until tender. Pour juices into a saucepan and boil down until syrupy. Swirl in a tablespoon or so of butter and pour over the celery.

MIREPOIX—DICED AROMATIC VEG-ETABLES. To give extra flavor to braised meats and vegetables. For about ⅓ cup. Sauté gently for about 10 minutes ¼ cup each finely diced carrots, onions, and celery in 2 tablespoons butter with a pinch of thyme and, if you wish, ¼ cup diced ham. When tender, season lightly to taste.

VARIATION

■ BRAISED LEEKS. Use 1 fat or 2 thin trimmed leeks per serving. Cut fat leeks in half lengthwise; leave thin ones whole. Place cut side up in one layer in a buttered baking dish, and proceed as for the braised celery, but omit the mirepoix.

Braised Endives

For 10 endives, to serve 5 to 10. Trim root ends of endives, keeping leaves attached. Arrange in one layer in a buttered flameproof casserole. Salt lightly, distribute 1½ tablespoons butter in small pieces on top, and sprinkle with 1 teaspoon lemon juice. Pour in water to come halfway up, and bring to the boil on top of the stove. Boil slowly for 15 minutes, or until almost tender. Lay buttered wax paper over the endives, cover the casserole, and bake in a 325°F oven for 1½ to 2 hours, or until the endives are a pale buttery yellow.

Sweet and Sour Red Cabbage

Serves 4 or 5. Sauté 1 cup red-onion slices in a large saucepan with 2 to 3 tablespoons of butter or oil or pork fat until tender. Blend in 4 cups of shredded red cabbage, a grated sour apple, 2 tablespoons red-wine vinegar, a puréed garlic clove, a bay leaf, 1/2 teaspoon caraway seeds, 1 teaspoon sugar, salt, pepper, and 1/2 cup water. Cover and boil over high heat for about 10 minutes, tossing occasionally and adding more water if necessary, until cabbage is tender and liquid has evaporated. Taste, and adjust seasonings.

POTATOES

Mashed Potatoes

For 2 1/2 pounds (4 or 5) large russet or Yukon-gold potatoes, to serve 6. Peel and quarter the potatoes, and boil for 10 to 15 minutes in salted water (1 1/2 teaspoons salt per quart) until definitely tender when pierced (but not overcooked!). Drain. Return to the pan and sauté for a minute or so to evaporate moisture. Either put through a potato ricer, or whip in an electric mixer at slow to medium speed, adding driblets of hot milk or cream. Season with salt and white pepper, beating in up to 1/2 cup in all of hot milk or cream by spoonfuls, and alternating with 1/2-tablespoon additions of butter. If not serving at once, set pan over almost simmering water and cover loosely—the potatoes must have a little air circulation. They will keep thus an hour or more; stir up once in a while, adding a little more butter if you wish before serving.

VARIATION

■ GARLIC MASHED POTATOES. After mashing the potatoes, purée a head or two of braised garlic cloves simmered in cream (see box), beat it into the potatoes, and proceed to season them, adding milk or cream and butter to taste. (In my early TV versions I used a more complicated system with a roux and so forth, but this is far simpler and better.)

GARLIC

GARLIC FACTOIDS. To separate the cloves from the head of garlic, cut off the top, then bang down on the head with your fist or the flat of a knife. To peel whole garlic cloves, drop them into a pan of boiling water and boil exactly 30 seconds; the peels will slip off easily. To mince garlic, smash a whole garlic clove on your work surface, peel off and discard the skin, then mince with your big knife. To purée, sprinkle a big pinch of salt on the minced garlic, then press and rub the garlic back and forth on your work surface with the flat of your knife, or pound with a mortar and pestle.

To remove garlic smell from your hands, wash in cold water, rub with salt, wash in soap and warm water; repeat if necessary.

BRAISED WHOLE CLOVES OF GARLIC. Simmer 1 head of large peeled garlic cloves and 1 tablespoon of butter or olive oil in a small covered saucepan for 15 minutes or so, until very tender but not browned.

BRAISED GARLIC CLOVES SIMMERED IN CREAM. Simmer the above braised garlic cloves with ½ cup of cream for about 10 minutes, until meltingly tender. Season with salt and white pepper.

Steamed Whole Potatoes

For small red-skinned or new potatoes about 2 inches in diameter. Scrub potatoes and, if you wish, peel off a band of skin around middle. Pile in a steamer basket set in a saucepan over 2 inches of water. Bring to a boil, cover closely, and steam 20 minutes or so, until easily pierced. Serve as is with seasonings and melted butter, or peel and slice for salad.

Boiled Sliced Potatoes

Especially for use in salads. For about 1 quart. Choose "boiling" potatoes all the same size. One at a time, peel them, cut into slices ¼ inch thick, and drop into cold water—to prevent discoloration. When all are done, drain and add fresh water to cover and 1½ teaspoons salt per quart. Simmer for 2 to 3 minutes, testing carefully to be sure they are tender. Drain, cover the pan, and let firm up for exactly 4 minutes, then uncover, and be prepared to season them while still warm.

Scalloped Potatoes—Gratin Dauphinois

For 2 pounds boiling potatoes, to serve 4 to 6. Wash potatoes, and one by one peel and cut into slices as described in the preceding recipe. Butter a flame-proof baking dish, smear bottom with a puréed clove of garlic, and lay in potato slices. Heat 1 cup of milk seasoned with salt and pepper, and pour over potatoes, adding milk if necessary to reach three-quarters of the way up. Bring to the simmer on top of the stove, and distribute 2 to 3 tablespoons butter in small pieces over potatoes. Bake in upper third of a preheated 425°F oven about 25 minutes, until the potatoes are tender and nicely browned on top.

VARIATIONS

▣ SCALLOPED POTATOES SAVOYARDE. Sauté 3 cups of thinly sliced onions in butter and prepare 1½ cups of grated Swiss cheese. Layer onions and cheese with the potato slices in the baking dish.

Instead of milk, heat 2 cups of well-seasoned chicken or beef stock; pour over potatoes to cover by three-quarters. Bake in 425°F oven, basting several times with the juices, until liquid is absorbed and potatoes are nicely browned, about 40 minutes.

■ POTATOES ANNA—SCALLOPED POTATOES BAKED IN BUTTER. For 2 pounds boiling potatoes, to serve 4 to 6. Prepare the potato slices as described above and dry well. Pour clarified butter (see box) into a 10-inch nonstick frying pan to a depth of ¼ inch; set over moderate heat and rapidly fill pan bottom with a layer of potato slices, overlapping in concentric circles. Shake pan to prevent sticking, baste first layer with a sprinkling of butter, and arrange the remaining slices in neat layers, sprinkling on butter after each, and seasoning with salt and pepper every few layers. When pan is filled, let cook 3 to 5 minutes to crust bottom layer. Lower heat, cover pan, and cook for 45 minutes, or until potatoes are easily pierced, making sure bottom does not burn. Loosen galette around the sides and invert onto a hot serving dish.

Sautéed Diced Potatoes

For 1½ pounds boiling potatoes, to serve 4. Peel the potatoes and cut into ¾-inch cubes; drop into cold water to remove starch. Drain, and dry on towels. Sauté over high heat in 3 tablespoons clarified butter (see box), or 2 tablespoons butter and 1 tablespoon oil, tossing frequently until nicely browned. Lower heat; season lightly with salt, pepper, and, if you wish, Provençal herbs (see box, p. 44). Cover and cook 3 or 4 minutes, until tender. If not serving at once, keep warm for 15 minutes or so, uncovered. To serve, raise heat to moderately high, then toss in a spoonful of chopped shallots and parsley, plus a tablespoon or so more of butter. Toss again for several minutes, and serve.

CLARIFIED BUTTER—FOR SAUTÉING. The simple system: melt the butter and pour the clear yellow liquid off the milky residue. The professional, long-keeping method: bring the butter to the slow boil in a roomy saucepan and boil until its crackling and bubbling almost cease; pour the clear yellow butter through a tea strainer into a jar, where it will keep for months in the refrigerator or freezer.

The Best Grated Potato Pancakes

This is my version of those wonderful ones Sally Darr used to serve in the sixties in her charming New York restaurant, La Tulipe. For 3 or 4 large-size baking potatoes, serving 6. Steam the potatoes 15 to 20 minutes, until almost but not quite tender. Set aside for several hours, until completely cold. Then peel and rub through the large holes of a hand grater. Toss with a sprinkling of salt and pepper and divide loosely into 6

Getting a laugh out of lobster

Opposite page, top:
Know where your meat comes from.

Opposite page bottom:
Serve a hearty, dry white wine or a simple red with your bouillabaisse.

This page, top:
Unmolding the omelet

This page, bottom:
Enjoying a talk with Professor Raymond Calvel on making French baguettes

Spooning up a luscious hollandaise

mounds. Film a frying pan with $1/8$ inch of clarified butter (see box), and when butter is hot, spread in 2 or 3 mounds, pressing the potatoes together lightly with a spatula for 4 to 5 minutes. Sauté for several minutes, until browned on the bottom, turn with care, and brown on the other side. Set aside uncovered, and reheat briefly in a 425°F oven.

VARIATION

▉ LARGE POTATO GALETTE. Form the potatoes into one large cake and sauté in a large nonstick frying pan. When bottom has browned, either flip it over, or slide out onto a baking sheet and plop it browned side up back into the pan to brown on the other side.

French Fries

For 3 pounds (4 or 5) baking potatoes about 5 inches long and $2^{1}/_{2}$ inches across, serving 6. Trim potatoes into even rectangles and cut into strips $3/8$ inch wide. Swish in cold water to remove surface starch. Just before frying, drain and dry thoroughly. Heat $2^{1}/_{2}$ quarts fresh frying oil (I use Crisco) to 325°F. Fry the equivalent of $1^{1}/_{2}$ potatoes at a time for 4 to 5 minutes, until cooked through but not browned. Drain, and spread out on paper towels. Let cool at least 10 minutes (or up to 2 hours). Just before serving, heat oil to 375°F and fry, again by handfuls, for a minute or two, to brown nicely. Remove and drain on paper towels. Salt lightly, and serve at once.

RICE

Plain Boiled White Rice

For 3 cups. Measure 1 cup plain white rice into a heavy-bottomed saucepan; stir in 2 cups cold water, 1 teaspoon salt, and 1 to 2 tablespoons butter or good olive oil. Bring to the boil over high heat and stir well; reduce heat to slow simmer, cover pan tightly, and cook undisturbed for 12 minutes—8 minutes for fat Italian Arborio. The rice is done when the liquid is completely absorbed and steam holes are visible on the surface. The rice will be almost tender, with the slightest

crunch in the center. Let sit 5 minutes off the heat, covered, to finish cooking. Then fluff with a wooden fork, and correct seasoning.

VARIATIONS

▉ BRAISED RICE—RISOTTO (FRENCH STYLE). Sauté $1/4$ cup of finely minced onion in 2 tablespoons of butter to soften. Stir in 1 cup of rice and cook, stirring with a wooden fork, for 2 to 3 minutes, until grains look milky. Stir in 2 tablespoons dry white French vermouth and 2 cups chicken stock, add 1 imported bay leaf, and bring to simmer. Season lightly. Stir once, lower heat, cover, and cook as for basic boiled rice.

■ BRAISED WILD RICE. For 1½ cups rice, making 4 cups cooked, serving 6 to 8. To clean and tenderize the rice, thoroughly wash and drain it, then boil for 10 to 15 minutes in 4 cups of water, until softened but still a little hard at the center. Drain, and wash again in cold water. Then proceed as for the preceding braised rice, but substitute ¼ cup mirepoix (see box, page 33) or mushroom duxelles (page 32) for the onions. When tender, sauté in its pan, stirring with a wooden fork, to evaporate moisture and crisp the rice lightly, adding, if you wish, another tablespoon or so of butter.

DRIED BEANS

Dried Beans Preliminary— the Quick Soak

Pick over 1 cup of dried beans, removing any debris, wash thoroughly, and bring to the boil in 3 cups of water. Boil exactly 2 minutes, cover, and set aside for exactly 1 hour. The beans and their liquid are now ready for cooking.

Open-Pot Bean Cookery

For 1 cup dried beans, making 3 cups, serving 4 to 6. Add to the preceding beans and their liquid a medium herb bouquet (see box, page 58), a peeled medium onion and carrot, and, if you wish, a 2-inch square of blanched salt pork (see box, page 60). Season lightly with salt, and simmer, partially covered, for 1 to 1½ hours, or until tender.

Pressure Cooker Beans

Using the same ingredients as for the preceding open-pot beans, bring to 15 pounds pressure for exactly 3 minutes. Remove from heat and let pressure go down by itself—10 to 15 minutes.

Crock-Pot or Slow-Cooker Beans

No presoaking is necessary. Just put the raw, unsoaked beans and other ingredients into the Crock-Pot at 6 p.m. and turn to "low"; they should be perfectly done the next morning. (Or set them in a covered casserole and bake in a 250°F oven overnight.)

Meats, Poultry, and Fish

"Meats, poultry, and fish—each is unique, but so many of them cook in almost the same way."

SAUTÉING

The quickest and easiest way to cook a ½-inch-thick single-portion size of meat, chicken, or fish is to sauté it, meaning you pat it dry, plop it into a hot pan, and cook it rapidly on one side, then the other, until it is nicely browned and just done. The meat juices caramelize in the pan, and that gives you the basis for your quick and delicious little pan sauce. If the portion is a bit thicker, it simply needs longer cooking, and you cover the pan to finish it off. Different foods demand, of course, slightly different treatments, and we'll start with the basic sauté, then go on to some of the essential variations.

FOR A SUCCESSFUL SAUTÉ

DRY THE FOOD. If the food is damp it will steam rather than brown. Pat it dry it in paper towels, or in some cases season it and dredge in flour just before cooking.

HEAT THE PAN. Set the pan over high heat, add the butter or oil, and wait until the butter foam is beginning to subside, or until your fat or oil is almost smoking. Then, and only then, add the food. If it is not really hot, the food will not brown.

DON'T CROWD THE PAN. Be sure there is a little space between pieces of food—about ¼ inch. If the pieces are crowded together, they will steam rather than brown. Don't fall into the trap of adding too much to your pan. Sauté in 2 or even 3 batches if necessary, or you'll be sorry.

THE FRYING PAN. Get yourself a good solid pan, one that will just hold your food and is neither too big nor too small. I am wedded to my trusty all-purpose professional-weight Wearever aluminum nonstick with its 10-inch top diameter, 8-inch bottom, and long handle. I also have the smaller size, 6 inches across, and the larger, 12-inch pan.

NOTE: This is not a fancy "gourmet" type pan, and you'll most often find it in a hardware store.

Sautéed Beef Steaks *Serves 4*

1 Tbs unsalted butter
1 tsp light olive oil or vegetable oil—a
    little more if needed
4 well-trimmed 5-to-6-ounce beefsteaks
    ½ inch thick (boneless loin strip, rib,
    or other)
Salt and freshly ground pepper

For the Deglazing Sauce

1 Tbs minced shallot or scallion
1 clove garlic, puréed, optional
⅔ cup red wine—or ½ cup dry white
    French vermouth
⅓ cup beef or chicken broth
1 to 2 Tbs unsalted butter

Set your frying pan over highest heat
and swirl in the butter and oil. When
the butter foam has almost subsided,
rapidly lay in the steaks. Sauté undisturbed for a minute or so, quickly
season the surface of the meat with salt
and pepper, and turn the steaks. Season
the steaks on the exposed sides, and let
brown again for a minute or so before
testing for doneness.

WHEN IS IT DONE? Test rapidly and
often, since meat can overcook very
quickly. Press it with your finger. If it
feels squashy, like raw meat, it is very
rare. As it cooks it becomes springy—
when lightly springy it is medium, and
if there is no spring it is well done.

The Deglazing Sauce. Remove the
meat to a hot platter and cover while
making the sauce. Tilt the pan and
spoon out all but a smidgen of fat, stir
in the shallot and garlic with a wooden
spoon, and let sauté a moment, then
swish in the wine and broth, stirring the
coagulated meat juices into the liquid.
Let boil rapidly for a few seconds, until
reduced to a syrup. Remove pan from
heat, toss in the butter, and swirl the pan
by its handle to swish the butter into the
sauce until it has been absorbed. The
sauce will smooth and thicken lightly;
you will have but a small spoonful of
deliciously concentrated juices per
person. Pour over the steaks, and serve.

VARIATIONS

■ VEAL SCALLOPS. Use 5-to-6-ounce
veal steaks (slices from the loin or leg)
½ inch thick. Season and brown on both
sides in hot butter and oil, as described
in the master recipe. Cook to medium—
until lightly springy to the touch.
Deglaze the pan with minced shallots,
white wine, a dash of dry Madeira or
port, and a sprinkling of tarragon.

■ BONELESS CHICKEN BREASTS. For a
quick sauté, I like to remove the skin and
pound the breast meat between sheets of
plastic wrap to a thickness of ½ inch.
Season with salt and pepper, then proceed
to the sauté in clarified butter (page 36).
Cook the breasts about 1 minute per

side, until springy to the touch—careful not to overcook, but you must be sure the chicken is cooked to the just-well-done stage—the juices run clear yellow with no tinge of pink. Deglaze the pan as described, with minced shallots, dry white French vermouth, and chicken stock; a sprinkling of tarragon goes nicely in the sauce here.

■ SHRIMP IN LEMON AND GARLIC. Sauté 30 "large medium" peeled and deveined raw shrimp in 3 tablespoons olive oil with 1 or 2 large cloves of garlic, minced, and the minced zest (yellow part of peel) of ½ lemon. When the shrimp have curled, in 2 minutes or so, and feel springy, remove from heat and toss with 2 tablespoons fresh lemon juice, drops of soy sauce, and salt and pepper to taste. Toss again, with 2 tablespoons of fine fresh olive oil and a sprinkling of minced parsley and fresh dill.

■ SEA SCALLOPS SAUTÉED WITH GARLIC AND HERBS. For 1½ pounds, serving 6. Cut large scallops in thirds or quarters. Season with salt and pepper and, the moment before cooking, dredge in flour (see box, page 42). Heat 2 to 3 tablespoons of clarified butter (see box, page 36) or olive oil in a large nonstick frying pan, and when very hot but not smoking, turn them into the pan. Toss every few seconds, swirling the pan by its handle. As they rapidly begin to brown add a large clove of minced garlic and 1½ tablespoons of minced shallots, then 2 tablespoons of minced fresh parsley. The scallops are done when just springy to the touch. Serve at once.

JUICE-EXUDING PROBLEMS? The scallops you buy may well have been "plumped" in a saline solution that exudes when the scallops are warmed, making a proper sauté impossible. If you are dealing with a fishmonger, always ask for "dry" scallops. In any case, it's wise to test them out by briefly heating through 3 or 4 in a dry nonstick frying pan. If liquid exudes, heat all of them by handfuls, drain—saving liquid for fish stock—dry, and then proceed to your sauté but cut down on the normal timing.

■ HAMBURGERS. Sometimes I like my hamburgers perfectly plain and at other times I want to flavor them. In any case, form the meat rather loosely into 5-ounce patties—about ½ inch thick for quick cooking.

Plain Hamburgers. If I'm to pan-fry them I rub the pan itself with a little vegetable oil, heat it to almost smoking, and sauté the hamburgers about 1 minute on each side. I give them the finger test, as in the master recipe—I like mine medium rare, when they are barely beginning to take on a little spring.

Rather than pan-frying plain hamburgers, however, I do recommend the stovetop grill pan with its ridged interior. Oil it lightly, heat it until almost smoking, and on go the hamburgers. The cooking fat runs out of the meat and off the ridges into the valleys.

Flavored Hamburgers. For 4 hamburgers, fold into the meat 1 grated medium-size onion, salt and pepper, 3 tablespoons sour cream, and ½ teaspoon mixed herbs such as Italian or Provençal seasoning. Just before sautéing, turn the burgers in flour and shake off excess. Sauté on both sides in hot oil and make the sauce as directed in the master recipe.

TO DREDGE OR NOT TO DREDGE

Dredging the food in a light coating of flour before the sauté helps to hold the meat together and also gives it a light protective crusting. You will have little or no caramelization in the pan, and as to sauce you may simply want to make a browned butter, as for the fish fillets meunière below. Or, if you have a thicker piece of meat that needs further cooking, let it simmer in the wine and broth, and the flour coating will give you a lightly thickened sauce.

Calf's Liver and Onions

For 4 slices of liver, 5 ounces each and 3/8 inch thick. Slowly sauté 3 cups sliced onions in the butter and oil, and when tender and translucent raise the heat and let the onions brown lightly for several minutes. Remove them to a side dish. Just before sautéing it, season the liver and dredge lightly in flour, shaking off excess. Add a little more butter and oil to the pan, heat until the butter foam begins to subside, and sauté the liver for less than a minute on each side—it will get further cooking and is to be served medium rare. Remove the pan from heat, spread the cooked onions over the liver, and pour in ½ cup of red wine or dry white French vermouth. Blend ½ tablespoon of Dijon-type mustard into ¼ cup chicken broth, and blend into the rest of the liquid. Set over moderate heat and bring to the slow boil, basting the liver and onions with the sauce for a minute or two. The liver is done when just lightly springy to the touch.

Fillets of Sole Meunière

For 4 fillets up to ½ inch thick and 5 to 6 ounces each. Just before sautéing, season the fish with salt and pepper and turn in flour, shaking off excess. Heat the butter and oil in the pan until the butter foam begins to subside, lay in the fillets, and sauté for about a minute on each side, just until the fish begins to take on a light springiness to the touch. Do not overcook—if the fish flakes, it is overdone. Remove to a hot platter, and sprinkle a tablespoon of minced fresh parsley over the fish. Rapidly wipe the pan clean with paper towels (so flour residue will not speckle the butter to come—or use a fresh pan). Heat 2 tablespoons of unsalted butter in the pan, swishing it about and letting it brown lightly. Remove the pan from heat, squeeze in the juice of half a lemon, and, if you wish, toss in a spoonful of capers before spooning the hot butter over the fish.

Thick Pork Chops

When your meat is thicker than ½ inch, it takes longer to cook, which means you could be burning the outside before the inside is done. You have two choices. Either brown the meat on both sides and set it in its pan in a 375°F oven to finish cooking—which works very well for steaks, chops, and fish—or brown the meat over high heat, then cover-cook it to finish more slowly, as it simmers in its sauce.

For 4 pork chops about 1¼ inches thick. First give them a ½-hour dry marinade by rubbing in a little salt and pepper, allspice, and dried thyme. Dry them off and brown them on both sides. Then pour around them ¾ cup of dry white vermouth, ½ cup of chicken broth, and 2 tablespoons of minced shallots. Cover the pan and let simmer slowly, basting rapidly every 4 to 5 minutes, until the meat is done to the medium stage—faintly pink. The best way to test is to make a slit in one chop close to the bone. Remove the chops to hot plates, and spoon excess fat out of the pan. Reduce the liquid to a syrup and pour over the chops.

Thick Veal Chops

Cook them the same way as the pork chops, but omit the spice marinade. A bit of tarragon would go nicely in the simmering liquid, and it will want a swish of butter after it has reduced to its sauce consistency.

Sauté of Beef Tenderloin

Cut the meat into 2-inch chunks—you will probably want 3 chunks, or about 6 ounces, per serving. After drying them off, toss and brown them on all sides for several minutes in hot butter and oil, until beginning to take on springiness to the touch—they should remain rare. Remove to a side dish and season with salt and pepper. Deglaze the pan with ¼ cup of dry Madeira or port, and pour in ½ cup of heavy cream. Return the meat to the pan. Bring to the simmer for a very few minutes, basting meat with the sauce as it thickens lightly. Serve on hot plates and decorate with sprigs of fresh parsley.

Sauté of Pork Tenderloin

Use the same system for pork tenderloin, but give it the dry-spice marinade suggested for the thick pork chops above. You may wish to omit the cream finish, using chicken stock instead.

Chicken Sautéed in White Wine

For 2½ to 3 pounds of chicken parts, serving 4 people. Brown the chicken pieces on all sides in hot butter and oil. Remove the wings and breasts, which need less cooking. Season legs and thighs, cover the pan, and continue to cook over moderate heat for another 10 minutes, turning once. Season the white meat and return it to the pan. Stir in 1 tablespoon minced shallots, ⅔ cup chicken broth, ½ cup dry white wine or vermouth, and ½ teaspoon dried tarragon or Provençal herbs (see box). Cover the pan and cook at the slow simmer 5 to 6 minutes more, turn, and baste the chicken pieces with pan juices, then continue cooking until tender—about 25 minutes in all. Remove the chicken to a hot platter. Spoon off fat and boil down cooking liquid to reduce by half. Off heat, swirl in the enrichment butter, pour the sauce over the chicken, and serve.

WHEN IS THE CHICKEN DONE? The flesh of the drumsticks and thighs is just tender when pressed. The juices run clear yellow when the meat is pricked deeply—if there's no juice, you have overcooked it, but the chicken must be cooked through.

VARIATIONS

■ A PROVENÇAL ADDITION. After returning the white meat to the pan, stir in 2 cups of fresh tomato pulp, page 30, and continue with the recipe. When you have removed the chicken, boil down the sauce until thick and fine, and carefully correct seasoning.

■ CHICKEN PIPÉRADE. In a separate pan, sauté 1 cup of sliced onions in olive oil until tender then add 1 cup each of sliced red and green pepper and a large clove of garlic, minced. Sauté together for a moment. Add to the chicken when you return the white meat.

■ BONNE FEMME—ONIONS, POTA-TOES, AND MUSHROOMS. After removing the white meat, add to the dark meat 3 or 4 medium Yukon-gold potatoes, quartered and blanched, and 8 to 12 small white onions (page 28). Continue with the recipe. After returning the white meat, fold in 1½ cups of previously sautéed quartered fresh mushrooms, and finish the recipe.

PROVENÇAL HERBS—HERBES DE PROVENCE.—A mixture of ground dried herbs, such as bay, thyme, rosemary, and oregano.

BROILING

Broiling, where the heat comes from above, is of course the opposite of barbecuing, where the heat source comes from below. Broiling, however, has the advantage that you are more easily in control. If your broiler is so equipped, you can raise or lower the heat, or in any case you can move the food nearer or farther from the broiler element. In some instances you simply broil on both sides until the food is completely cooked, and in others you may find that broiling just on one side is sufficient. In still other cases, especially when you have something large like a butterflied roasting chicken, you will want to broil and brown the two sides but finish by roasting—very convenient when your oven is both broiler and roaster. There are no rules, and it is quite up to you to decide. Here are some examples.

MASTER RECIPE

Broiled Butterflied Chicken *Serves 4*

Rather than broiling a chicken in pieces, which is easy to do but not wildly exciting, and rather than roasting it whole, which takes an hour or more, butterfly your chicken. It cooks in half the time and makes a great presentation.

A 2½-to-3-pound broiler-fryer chicken, butterflied
2 Tbs melted butter blended with 2 tsp vegetable oil
Salt and freshly ground pepper
½ tsp dried thyme or an herb mixture

For the Deglazing Sauce

1 Tbs minced shallot or scallion
½ cup chicken broth and/or dry white wine or vermouth
1 to 2 Tbs butter, for enrichment

TO BUTTERFLY A CHICKEN. With heavy shears or a cleaver, cut down close to the backbone on each side, and remove the bone. Spread the chicken open, skin side up, and pound on the breast with your fist to flatten the chicken. Cut off and discard the little nubbins at the wing elbows, and fold the wings akimbo. To hold the legs in place, make ½-inch slits in the skin on each side of the lower breast and tuck the drumstick ends through the slits.

Preheat the broiler to high. Brush the chicken all over with butter and oil and arrange it skin side down in a shallow pan. Set it under the broiler so the chicken surface is about 6 inches from the heat source. Let broil for about 5 minutes, then baste rapidly with the butter and oil, and continue for another 5 minutes. The surface should be browning nicely; if not, adjust the heat or the distance of chicken from broiler. Baste again, this time with the juices accumulated in the pan, and broil another 5 minutes. Then season with salt and pepper, turn the chicken skin side up, and season the surface. Continue broiling and basting with the pan juices every 5 minutes for another 10 to 15 minutes, until the chicken is done (see box, page 44).

Remove the chicken to a carving board and let it rest for 5 minutes. Meanwhile, make the deglazing sauce by first spooning cooking fat off the juices in the pan. Then stir the shallot into the pan and simmer for a minute or so on top of the stove, until the juices are syrupy. Swirl in the enrichment butter, pour over the chicken, and serve.

VARIATIONS

■ **BROIL/ROASTED BUTTERFLIED ROASTING CHICKEN—AND TURKEY.** Broil/roasting a big 6-to-7-pound butterflied roaster or capon or a 12-pound turkey takes, again, half the time you'd need if you roasted it whole. Use exactly the same system as for the preceding broiled chicken except that, when you have browned the underside, and given the skin side the beginning of a brown, you then switch from broiling to roasting. Just finish the cooking in the oven— I like to roast mine at 350°F. A 6-to-7-pound bird takes 1 to 1¼ hours; a 12-pound turkey, about 2 hours. See the broil/roast times box for more details.

BROIL/ROAST CHICKEN AND TURKEY TIMES

Always allow an additional 20 to 30 minutes, just to be safe.
Butterflied Roasting Chickens
  4 to 5 pounds / 45 minutes to 1 hour
  5 to 6 pounds / 1 to 1¼ hours
Butterflied Turkeys
  8 to 12 pounds / 1½ to 2 hours
  12 to 16 pounds / 2 to 2½ hours
  16 to 20 pounds / 2½ to 3 hours

■ **DEVILED GAME HENS OR POUSSINS.** For 2 birds, serving 4 people. Butterfly the birds and broil as in the master recipe, but give them only 10 minutes per side. Meanwhile, whisk together, to make a mayonnaise-like sauce, ⅓ cup Dijon mustard, a large minced shallot, pinches of dried tarragon or rosemary, drops of Tabasco sauce, and 3 tablespoons of the pan juices. Paint this over the skin sides of the birds, then pat on a layer of fresh white bread crumbs. Baste with the remaining juices. Finish cooking under the broiler.

FRESH BREAD CRUMBS. Whenever bread crumbs are called for, always make your own out of fresh homemade-type bread. Cut off the crusts, slice the bread into 1-inch chunks, and pulse not more than 2 cups at a time in a food processor, or 1 cup at a time in an electric blender. It's useful to make a lot while you are at it and freeze what you don't need.

Broiled Fish Steaks—About ¾ Inch Thick

For salmon, swordfish, tuna, bluefish, shark, mahimahi, and so forth. Here you concentrate on browning the top of the fish; no need to turn it. Dry the fish, paint both sides with melted butter or vegetable oil, and season with salt and pepper. Arrange in a shallow pan that will just hold them comfortably. Pour around the steaks ⅛ inch of dry white wine or French vermouth and set 2 inches below a preheated broiler. After 1 minute, brush a little soft butter on top of each and squeeze on drops of lemon juice. Continue broiling about 5 minutes more, or until lightly springy to the touch—cooked through but still juicy. Serve with the cooking juices spooned over.

VARIATIONS

■ THICK FISH STEAKS—1 TO 2 INCHES THICK. Broil to brown them nicely, then finish off in a 375°F oven.

■ FISH FILLETS. For such fish as salmon, cod, hake, mackerel, trout. Leave the skin on, to keep the fish in shape during cooking, and follow directions for the preceding fish steaks.

Lamb Brochettes

Cut roasting-quality lamb, such as leg or loin, into 1½-inch chunks. You may wish to marinate them for several hours or overnight, as suggested below; otherwise, season and oil the meat. Thread onto skewers, alternating each piece with a square of blanched bacon (see box on page 60) and a piece of imported bay leaf. Arrange on an oiled broiling pan or in a hinged rack. Broil 2 inches from heat, turning every 2 minutes for several minutes, until the meat is just springy to the touch.

HERB AND LEMON MARINADE FOR LAMB OR BEEF. Here is a basic formula that you may vary as you wish. For every 2 pounds of meat, mix the following in a bowl: 2 tablespoons freshly squeezed lemon juice, 1 tablespoon soy sauce, 1 teaspoon ground rosemary, thyme, oregano, or Provençal herbs (see box, page 44), 2 large cloves puréed garlic, and ¼ cup vegetable oil.

OILS—FOR COOKING, FLAVORING, AND SALADS. Use fresh-tasting, neutral-flavored oils for cooking, such as light olive, canola, or other vegetable oils. Olive oils for flavoring and salads can be mild or fruity, and since they have become a status symbol, you can pay enormous prices for some of those labeled "extra virgin." Test them out yourself to find the brand or brands that suit you.

NOTE: "EVOO" is contemporary cook talk for "extra virgin olive oil."

Broiled Flank Steak

To keep the meat in shape while cooking, lightly score the surface (cut crosshatches 1/8 inch deep) on each side with the point of your small, sharp knife. Give it the marinade treatment if you wish (see box, page 47), for 1/2 hour up to a day or two; or season with salt, pepper, and a little soy sauce, and brush with vegetable oil. Set close under the broiler for 2 to 3 minutes on each side, until just beginning to take on springiness to the touch—for rare. To serve, cut into thin, slanting slices across the grain.

Broiled Hamburgers

Prepare them as described for sautéed hamburgers (page 42) but omit the flour coating. Brush with cooking oil and set close under the hot broiler for 1 to 2 minutes on each side—when just beginning to take on springiness to the touch, they are medium rare. You might want to top them with one of the flavored butters noted in the box on page 49.

Butterflied Leg of Lamb

Half an hour or the day before cooking, trim off excess fat and spread the lamb out skin side down. Make lengthwise slashes in the 2 large lobes of meat and spread out to even the mass. Brush the flesh side with the meat marinade (see box, page 47), or season with salt, pepper, and rosemary or Provençal herbs (see box, page 44), and oil both sides.

Set 7 to 8 inches under the hot broiler element and brown nicely for about 10 minutes on each side, basting with oil. (Browning may be completed an hour or so in advance. See box.) Finish in a 375°F oven, roasting for 15 to 20 minutes to a meat-thermometer reading of 140°F for medium rare. Let rest 10 to 15 minutes before carving, which allows the meat juices to return to the flesh.

BROIL/ROASTING AHEAD OF TIME. For a large piece of meat, like a butterflied roasting chicken or a boned and butterflied leg of lamb or pork loin, you can do the preliminary browning somewhat in advance. Cover loosely and leave at room temperature, then finish it off later.

Roast/Broiled Butterflied Pork Loin

Here you roast it first, until almost done, then finish it off under the broiler to brown and crisp the surface. For 8 people, buy yourself a 3½-pound boneless pork-loin roast and untie it; it is already butterflied. Remove excess fat but leave a 1/4-inch layer on top. Slash the thick sections of meat lengthwise to even it out, and rub the meat either with dry spice marinade (see box, page 49), or with salt, pepper, allspice, and pulverized imported bay leaf. Oil the meat, cover, and refrigerate overnight. Roast it fat side up for about an hour at 375°F, to a meat-thermometer reading of 140°F. Half an hour before serving, make decorative cross-slashes in the fat side and rub in ½ tablespoon or so of coarse salt. Brown slowly under the broiler to an internal temperature of 162° to 165°F.

DRY SPICE MARINADE FOR PORK PRODUCTS, GOOSE, AND DUCK. Blend the following ground spices in a screw-topped jar and use ½ teaspoon per pound of meat. For about 1¼ cups: 2 tablespoons each of clove, mace, nutmeg, paprika, thyme, and imported bay; 1 tablespoon each of allspice, cinnamon, and savory; and 5 tablespoons white peppercorns.

SALT PROPORTIONS. In general, the proportion of salt to use in liquids is 1½ teaspoons per quart. The proportion of salt to raw meat is ¾ to 1 teaspoon per pound.

FLAVORED BUTTER TOPPING—FOR BROILED MEATS, FISH, CHICKEN. To make the standard *maître d'hôtel,* beat drops of lemon juice into a stick of softened unsalted butter, adding a teaspoon each of minced shallot and parsley, and salt and pepper to taste. Other alternatives or additions can be puréed garlic, anchovies, Dijon mustard, chives or other herbs, and so forth. Make a larger quantity, roll it into a sausage shape, wrap it, and freeze it; it is ready for instant use.

ROASTING

Roasting or baking means to cook food in the oven, usually in an open pan—sometimes with a cover, but not with a liquid. Roasting with a liquid is officially called braising or stewing. Roasting is certainly the most painless way of cooking a whole chicken or turkey, prime ribs of beef, legs of lamb, and so forth. Fortunately, a roast is a roast is a roast—all of them are done in much the same way. Give yourself plenty of time. Always preheat the oven at least 15 minutes before you begin, and start testing rapidly with your instant meat thermometer 10 to 15 minutes before the end of your estimated roasting time. Remember that the roast needs a 15-to-20-minute rest before carving, which allows the hot and bursting juices to retreat back into the meat. A large roast will stay warm a good 20 minutes at least before being carved, so plan accordingly. Note: All roasting times in this book are for conventional ovens.

Roast Prime Ribs of Beef *For a 3-rib 8-pound roast, serving 6 to 8 people*

Roasting time at 325°F: 2 hours for medium rare—internal temperature 125° to 130°F (about 15 minutes per pound).

1 Tbs vegetable oil
Salt and freshly ground pepper

For the Deglazing Sauce
½ cup each chopped carrots and onions
½ tsp dried thyme
½ cup chopped fresh plum tomatoes
2 cups beef broth

Preheat the oven to 325°F. Rub the exposed ends of the roast with oil and a sprinkling of salt. Arrange the roast rib side down in a roasting pan and set in the lower third of the preheated oven. After ½ hour, baste the ends of the roast with accumulated fat, strew the carrots and onions into the pan, and baste with the fat. Continue roasting, basting again once or twice, to a meat-thermometer reading of 125° to 130°F at the large end.

Remove the roast. Spoon fat out of the roasting pan. Stir in the thyme and tomatoes, scraping up coagulated roasting juices. Blend in the broth and boil several minutes to concentrate flavor. Correct seasoning, and strain into a warm sauceboat.

ROAST BEEF: SIZES AND APPROXIMATE ROASTING TIMES TO MEDIUM RARE (125° to 130°F)

5 ribs, 12 lbs / serves 12 to 16 / roasts about 3 hours at 325°F

4 ribs, 9½ lbs / serves 9 to 12 / roasts about 2 hours and 20 minutes at 325°F

3 ribs, 8 lbs, serves 6 to 8 / roasts about 2 hours at 325°F

2 ribs, 4½ lbs / serves 5 to 6 / roasts 15 minutes at 450°F, 45 minutes at 325°F

ROAST BEEF: TEMPERATURES AND MINUTES PER POUND

Rare, 120°F, 12 to 13 minutes per pound
Medium rare, 125° to 130°F, about 15 minutes per pound
Medium, 140°F, 17 to 20 minutes per pound

Roast Top Loin (New York Strip) of Beef

A boneless ready-to-roast 4½-pound strip serves 8 to 10. Timing: 1¼ to 1½ hours; roast at 425°F for 15 minutes, then at 350°F, to internal temperature 120°F for rare or 125°F for medium rare. (It's the circumference of the meat that dictates the timing; thus all lengths roast in about the same time—a little less or a little more, depending on weight.) Oil and salt the 2 exposed ends, and roast fat side up on an oiled rack, strewing ½ cup chopped onions and carrots in the pan halfway through. Make the sauce as suggested in the master recipe.

Roast Tenderloin of Beef

A boneless ready-to-roast 4-pound tenderloin of beef serves 6 to 8. Timing: 35 to 45 minutes at 400°F, to internal temperature 120°F for rare, or 125°F for medium rare. Just before roasting, salt the meat lightly and brush with clarified butter. Set in the upper-third level of the oven; rapidly turn and baste with clarified butter every 8 minutes. For sauce suggestions, see box at right.

> **SIMPLE HORSERADISH SAUCE— ESPECIALLY FOR ROAST BEEF.** Whisk 2 tablespoons Dijon mustard into 5 tablespoons bottled horseradish. Fold in 1/2 cup or so of sour cream, and salt and pepper to taste.

Roast Leg of Lamb

A 7-pound leg, hip and sirloin removed, weighs about 5 pounds and serves 8 to 10. Timing: about 2 hours in a 325°F oven to internal temperature 140°F for medium rare; to 125° to 130°F for rare; to 120°F for blood rare. Before roasting, you may wish to puncture the meat in a dozen places and push in slivers of garlic, then brush the surface with oil, or paint on a mustard coating (see box, page 52). Roast fat side up in a preheated oven as described in the master recipe, rapidly basting every 15 minutes with accumulated fat. After an hour, strew in 1/2 cup of chopped onions and several large cloves of smashed unpeeled garlic. Make the sauce as described in the master recipe, adding 1/2 teaspoon of rosemary, and 2 cups of chicken broth. See also the box below for other suggestions.

> **A SIMPLE SAUCE FOR LAMB.** Have the lamb hip- and tailbones (plus other lamb bones or scraps if available) chopped or sawed into 1/2-inch pieces, and brown with a little oil in a heavy pan with a chopped carrot, onion, and celery stalk. Sprinkle on a tablespoon of flour and brown, stirring for a minute or two. Add a chopped plum tomato, an imported bay leaf, and a big pinch of rosemary, plus chicken broth and water to cover. Simmer slowly, loosely covered, for 2 hours, adding more liquid as needed. Strain, degrease, and boil down to concentrate flavor. Use this plus 1/2 cup of dry white wine to make your deglazing sauce.
>
> *Simple Sauce for Meat and Poultry.* Follow the same general system as above for other meat and poultry sauces, using beef or poultry bones and scraps, other herbs, and beef rather than chicken broth, as appropriate.
>
> *Port or Madeira Sauce.* Use exactly the same system, substituting dry port or Madeira wine for the dry white wine.

LEG OF LAMB NOTES. Whether you buy the whole leg, the shank end, or the sirloin end, you roast it in the same way. The leg is much easier to carve when the hip- and tailbones have been removed. Don't buy a whole leg weighing more than 7½ pounds unless you know it has been properly aged—otherwise it can be unpleasantly tough.

Imported Legs of Lamb (New Zealand, Iceland, etc.)

These are smaller, younger, and tenderer than most American lamb. Either roast at 325°F as described above, counting on 25 minutes per pound, or, since they are so tender, you may wish to roast them at 400°F, counting on an hour or less.

Rack of Lamb

Two racks serve 4 or 5 people, 2 to 3 chops each. If the racks have not been "frenched," scrape off the fatty meat between the ribs and from the chop bones. Score the fat side of the ribs lightly and paint with mustard coating (see box). Roast for 10 minutes at 500°F, sprinkle ½ cup fresh bread crumbs (page 46) over the meat, and drizzle on a little melted butter. Roast 20 minutes more, or to internal temperature 125°F, for red rare, a little longer, to 140°F, for medium rare. Let rest 5 minutes before cutting into 1-rib chops.

HERBAL GARLIC AND MUSTARD COATING. Whisk together to a mayonnaise-like consistency ⅓ cup Dijon mustard with 3 large cloves of puréed garlic, 1 tablespoon soy sauce, ½ teaspoon ground rosemary, and 3 tablespoons light olive oil. Spread all over your leg of lamb and let marinate ½ hour or cover and refrigerate several hours or overnight. If you use this, no basting is necessary and you will have few if any roasting juices; you may wish to make a separate sauce, as described on page 51.

Roast Loin of Pork

For a 4-pound boneless roast, serving 8 to 10. Roasting time: 2¼ to 2½ hours at 350°F, to internal temperature 160°F. Buy the center cut of the loin, folded in two and tied fat side out to make a roast about 5 inches in circumference. I highly recommend the spice marinade in the box on page 49. To use it, untie the roast and rub it all over with the mixture, using ¼ teaspoon per pound. Lightly score the fat side and retie. Cover and refrigerate for an hour or up to 48 hours. Roast, basting occasionally, as for the master recipe, and after 1½ hours strew into the pan ½ cup each of chopped carrots and onions and 3 large cloves of smashed unpeeled garlic. Make the sauce as described, or prepare a port-wine sauce (see box, page 51).

■ ROAST FRESH HAM (LEG OF FRESH POR K). A 7-to-8-pound boneless leg serves 20 to 24. Timing: about 3½ hours, at 425°F for 15 minutes and then at 350°F, to internal temperature 160°F. A preroasting marinade is recommended: untie the pork and give it a 2-day spice marinade, as described for the pork loin, then retie. After browning the roast for 15 minutes, protect the areas not covered by fat by draping 8 to 10 strips of blanched bacon (see box, page 60) over the meat. Continue roasting at 350°F as described for the pork loin, strewing in the vegetables after 2½ hours. Remove the bacon strips the last ½ hour. The port wine sauce (see box, page 51) would go nicely here.

■ BAKED SMOKED HAM AND SHOULDER. These come fully or partially cooked. Follow the directions on the label for baking them. I prefer to braise them in wine, as described on page 59.

Meat Loaf

Whether you roast it freeform in the oven or bake it in a loaf pan, meat loaf is certainly an all-time favorite, as, in France, is its cousin the pâté. Since they are so closely related, I consider the one a variation of the other and here are two of my favorites.

BEEF AND PORK MEAT LOAF. For a 2-quart loaf serving 12, sauté 2 cups of minced onions in 2 tablespoons of oil until tender and translucent, raise heat and brown lightly. Toss in a bowl with 1 cup fresh bread crumbs (see box, page 46), 2 pounds ground beef chuck, 1 pound ground pork shoulder, 2 eggs, ½ cup beef broth, ⅔ cup grated cheddar cheese, 1 large clove puréed garlic, 2 teaspoons salt, ½ teaspoon pepper, 2 teaspoons each of thyme and paprika, 1 teaspoon each of allspice and oregano. To check seasoning, sauté a spoonful. Pack into a buttered 2-quart loaf pan and top with 2 imported bay leaves. Bake about 1½ hours at 350°F until juices run almost clear yellow and loaf is lightly springy to the touch.

Serve hot with tomato sauce, page 30, or let cool and then chill.

■ FRENCH-STYLE COUNTRY PÂTÉ. For a 6-cup loaf pan serving 8 to 10. Sauté ⅔ cup minced onions in 2 tablespoons butter until tender and translucent. Blend with 1¼ pounds pork sausage meat, ¾ pound ground chicken breast, ½ pound pork liver or beef liver, 1 cup fresh bread crumbs (see box, page 46), 1 egg, ⅓ cup goat cheese or cream cheese, 1 medium clove puréed garlic, 3 tablespoons cognac, 1 tablespoon salt, ¼ teaspoon each ground allspice, thyme, imported bay, and pepper. Sauté a spoonful to check seasoning. Pack into a buttered loaf pan and cover with wax paper and foil. Set in a larger pan of boiling water and bake 1¼ to 1½ hours, until juices are almost pale yellow.

Let repose for an hour, then set a board or twin pan on top and a 5-pound weight (like canned goods). When cool, cover and chill. Let "cure" for a day or two before serving.

Roast Chicken

A 3½-to-4-pound chicken serves 4 or 5 people. Timing: 1 hour and 10 to 20 minutes, at 425°F for 15 minutes and then at 350°F, to internal temperature of 170°F. See box below. Before roasting, wash the chicken rapidly in hot water and dry thoroughly. For ease in carving, cut out the wishbone. Season inside the cavity with salt and pepper and, if you wish, a thinly sliced lemon, a small onion, and a handful of celery leaves. Salt the chicken lightly all over and rub with soft butter. Tie drumstick ends together, and set breast up in an oiled V-shaped rack (or fold wings akimbo and set on an oiled flat rack). After its 15-minute browning in the hot oven, reduce heat to 350°F, baste rapidly with accumulated pan juices, and continue, basting rapidly every 8 to 10 minutes. After ½ hour, strew ½ cup each of chopped carrots and onions into the pan, basting them. When the chicken is done, make the sauce as described in the master recipe.

WARNING: Because of possibly harmful bacteria in raw chicken, be sure to wash all utensils and surfaces the chicken may have touched.

WHEN IS A ROAST CHICKEN DONE? When an instant meat thermometer inserted between the thigh and breast reads 165°–170°F, its legs move in their sockets, the thickest part of the drumstick is tender when pressed, and when it is pricked deeply its juices run clear yellow. When you hold the chicken breast-up, the very last drops of juice to drain from the vent run clear yellow.

GIBLETS—THE LIVER, GIZZARD, AND NECK. Use the gizzard and neck for making light chicken stock (page 4). Tuck the liver inside the cavity and let it roast with the chicken, or save it in your freezer to make chicken-liver sauté or a French pâté.

TIMING FOR ROAST CHICKEN. Count on a basic 45 minutes plus 7 minutes per pound. In other words, a 3-pound chicken takes the basic 45 plus (7 × 3) 21, which equals 66 minutes, or just over an hour.

VARIATIONS

■ **ROAST POUSSINS AND GAME HENS.** About 1 pound each. Prepare them as for the preceding chicken, but roast them for 35 to 45 minutes in a 425°F oven, basting rapidly several times.

■ **ROAST TURKEY.** Count on ½ pound of turkey per serving, or 1 pound per person, with leftovers. Roast at 325°F (see box below for high-temperature roasting). Timing for unstuffed birds: 12 to 14 pounds, about 4 hours; 16 to 20 pounds, about 5 hours; 20 to 26 pounds, about 6 hours. Add 20 to 30 minutes in all for stuffed birds. Internal temperatures: 175°F at the thickest portion of the leg; 165°F in the breast; 160°F in the center of the stuffing. Stuffing amounts are ½ to ¾ cup per pound of turkey, making roughly 2 to 2½ quarts of stuffing for a 14-to-16-pound bird. I frankly prefer a flavoring in the cavity, as suggested for the roast chicken, rather than a stuffing, and I cook the stuffing separately. Make turkey stock with the neck and scraps, as for chicken stock (page 4). Save the liver, heart, and gizzard for giblet gravy (see box, right). To prepare the turkey for roasting, cut out the wishbone and cut off the wing nubbins. Skewer the neck skin to the backbone, and skewer or sew the cavity closed or close it with foil. Rub the turkey with salt and vegetable oil. Roast breast up on an oiled rack, basting rapidly every 20 minutes or so. Start testing rapidly for doneness 20 minutes before the estimated roasting time—and note that a sure indication of approaching doneness is that turkey juices begin to exude into the pan.

WARNING: Do not stuff your turkey in advance, since the stuffing could start to sour and spoil inside the bird—goodbye, happy holidays.

DEFROSTING FROZEN TURKEY. Keep the turkey in its original wrapper. A 20-pound bird takes 3 to 4 days to defrost in the refrigerator, about 12 hours in a sinkful of water.

GIBLET GRAVY. Follow procedure for the simple sauce for meat and poultry (see box, page 51), browning the chopped turkey neck and scraps as described. Peel the gizzard and add it to simmer with the rest of the ingredients, removing it after about an hour, or when it is tender. Mince it. Sauté the heart and liver briefly in butter, mince them, and add to the finished sauce along with the minced gizzard, simmering for several minutes and adding, if you wish, a spoonful or so of dry port or Madeira.

HIGH-TEMPERATURE ROASTING. In my system, you start the roasting at 500°F, and in 15 to 20 minutes, when the juices begin to burn, reduce the heat to 450°F. Add the chopped vegetables and 2 cups of water to the pan, pouring in a little more water now and then as needed to prevent burning and smoking. A 14-pounder will roast in about 2 rather than 4 hours. High heat makes a brown and juicy turkey, but you have little control in such a hot oven, and I think the slower, longer cooking produces a more tender bird.

Steam-Roasted Duck

This is one of my favorite recipes, where you not only get rid of excess fat, but you get delicious breast meat, tender thighs, and beautifully crisp brown skin. Note that you may complete the final roasting an hour or so after the second, or braising, step.

For a 5-to-5½-pound roaster duckling serving 4. Cut out the wishbone, and chop off the wings at the elbows. Salt the interior and rub outside and inside with cut lemon. Place breast-up on a rack over 1 inch of water in a heavy, covered casserole and steam for 30 minutes on top of the stove. Drain the duck, pour out steaming liquid (degrease and save for stock). Cover the rack with foil and set the duck breast-down on it. Strew around ½ cup each of chopped onions, carrots, and celery, pour in 1½ cups of red or white wine. Cover closely and bring to the simmer, then braise for 30 minutes in a 325°F oven. Finally set the duck breast-up on a rack in a shallow pan and roast 30 to 40 minutes more at 375°F, until the legs feel reasonably tender. The skin will be beautifully brown and crisp. Meanwhile, degrease the braising juices, mash the vegetables into them, and boil down rapidly until almost syrupy. Strain, and you will have just enough fragrant sauce to moisten each serving.

Steam-Roasted Goose

For a 9½-to-11-pound roaster goose serving 8 to 10. Use essentially the same system as for duck, but give it a trussing by running a skewer through the carcass at the shoulder to secure the wings in place, and another through the hips to secure the legs, then tie the drumstick ends together against the tailpiece. To aid in fat removal prick the skin with a sharp skewer around the lower breast and thighs. Count on about 1 hour for the first breast-up steaming, 1½ to 2 hours for the oven braising, and 30 to 40 minutes for the final oven browning. Make the braising liquid as for the duck, but with 2½ cups of wine or chicken stock. You may wish to thicken it lightly at the end by simmering it for a few minutes with 1½ tablespoons of cornstarch blended with ½ cup of dry port wine.

Roast Whole Fish

For bass, bluefish, char, cod, mackerel, salmon, trout, and others. This is one of the simplest and easiest ways to cook a fairly large whole fish, which roasts deliciously in its own juices. Timing in a 400°F oven for a 6-to-8-pound fish is 35 to 45 minutes; 4 to 6 pounds, 25 to 30 minutes; 2 to 4 pounds, 15 to 20 minutes. Scale and eviscerate the fish, remove the gills, and trim the tail and fins with scissors. Sprinkle salt and pepper in the cavity and tuck in a handful of fresh parsley sprigs or dill weed. Brush the outside of the fish with vegetable oil and set on an oiled baking sheet. Roast in the middle level of the preheated oven until you can smell the juices beginning to exude, meaning the fish is done—the back fin can be easily pulled out, and there will be no bloody tinge in the cavity. Serve with lemon, melted butter, a butter sauce, or hollandaise (page 13).

VARIATION

▐ FOR SMALLER, MORE DELICATE FISH, LIKE TROUT AND SMALL MACKEREL. A 1-pound fish needs 15 to 20 minutes at 425°F. Prepare the fish as described, and brush it with oil or melted butter. Just before roasting, roll it in flour, shaking off excess, then roast it on an oiled baking sheet.

STEWING, BRAISING, AND POACHING

When food cooks in a liquid it is either stewed, braised, or poached. The first and simplest is the stew, typified by the pot-au-feu boiled dinner, where meat and aromatic vegetables simmer together in a big pot. Braising is more sophisticated, since the meat is first browned, then cooked in a fragrant liquid—beef bourguignon is the classic example here. Poaching is for fragile items like fillets of sole in white wine, where a small amount of liquid is at the barest simmer.

STEWING

MASTER RECIPE

Pot au Feu Boiled Dinner *Serves 8*

Cooking time: 2 to 4 hours, unsupervised.

2 quarts brown beef stock (page 5, and note that if you're making a stock, the beef can cook along with it), or beef bouillon and water

Optional, for additional flavor: any beef bones and scraps, cooked or raw

1 large herb bouquet (see box, page 58)

Aromatic vegetables, roughly chopped: 3 large peeled carrots, 3 large peeled onions, 1 large washed leek, 3 large celery ribs with leaves

About 5 pounds boneless stewing beef (or sufficient bone-in meat), such as heel of the round, foreshank, neck pot roast, chuck, brisket, short ribs—all one kind or a mixture

Vegetable garnish suggestions, any or all of the following: 2 or 3 pieces each of turnips (page 29), parsnips (page 29), carrots (page 29), small white onions (page 28), cabbage wedges (page 27), boiling potatoes (page 35).

Bring the stock to the boil in a large pot with the optional bones and scraps, the herb bouquet, and the aromatic vegetables. Meanwhile, tie the meat into a neat shape with white cotton twine, and place it in the pot, adding water if necessary to cover by 1 inch. Bring to the simmer, skim off surface scum for several minutes, then cover the pot loosely and let simmer slowly until the meat is tender when pierced with a fork—cut off and eat a piece to be sure. If some pieces are done early, remove to a bowl and cover with a little of the cooking stock. When the meat is done, remove it from the pot, strain and degrease the cooking stock, correct seasoning, and return it to the pot with the meat. The stew will keep warm for a good hour before serving, or may be reheated, loosely covered.

Meanwhile, cook separately whatever vegetables you have chosen in a bit of the cooking stock, and when you are ready to serve, drain their cooking liquids into a saucepan. Then add a sufficient quantity of the cooking liquid to make a rich stock to serve with your pot au feu. Slice the meat, surround with the vegetables, and baste with the stock, pouring the rest into a sauceboat to pass at the table. Accompany, if you wish, with French cornichons, coarse salt, and horseradish sauce (see box, page 51).

HERB BOUQUET. For a large herb bouquet, tie 8 parsley sprigs, 1 large imported bay leaf, 1 teaspoon dried thyme, 4 whole cloves or allspice berries, and 3 large cloves of smashed unpeeled garlic together in washed cheesecloth. Sometimes the garlic should be omitted, and you can substitute celery leaves and/or split leeks.

VARIATIONS

■ OTHER MEATS. Include or substitute other meats in the stew, such as shoulder of pork or veal, or Polish sausage. Or you may wish to use a fine stewing hen, which you can include with the beef or cook separately, in this latter case using chicken rather than beef stock.

■ BLANQUETTE OF VEAL. For 4 to 5 pounds of real pale-pink special-fed veal (see note, page 59) cut into 2-inch chunks (a combination of boneless and bone-in chuck, shank, neck, and breast), serving 6 people. Simmering time: about 1½ hours. Bring the veal to the simmer for 2 to 3 minutes in a large pot of water until the scum ceases to rise. Drain. Wash off the veal and the pot, return veal to pot, then pour in veal, chicken, or turkey stock (pages 4–5) or canned chicken broth and water to cover by ½ inch. Add a large peeled and chopped onion, a peeled chopped carrot, a large chopped celery stalk, and a small herb bouquet minus garlic (see box, page

58). Salt lightly, cover the pot loosely, and simmer about 1½ hours, until meat is fork-tender. Drain stock into a saucepan and return meat to pot. Degrease cooking liquid, and boil down rapidly until reduced to about 3 cups. Meanwhile, make a velouté sauce (page 13) with 4 tablespoons butter, 5 tablespoons flour, and the cooking liquid, enriching it, if you wish, with a little cream. Simmer the veal to warm briefly in the sauce along with 24 small white-braised onions (page 28) and ½ pound of small simmered mushrooms (page 32).

NOTE: "Real" veal is a calf either fed on mother's milk or on milk by-products. "Free-range" veal, which is actually "baby beef," produces an ugly gray-brown blanquette and an inferior sauce. It will, however, make an acceptable brown stew, using the following beef bourguignon system.

■ **BLANQUETTE OF CHICKEN OR TURKEY.** Use cut-up roasting or stewing chicken, or turkey parts, cooking them the same way.

BRAISING

In these recipes the meat is sautéed or browned before the actual cooking begins. Remember the rules for sautéing: the meat won't brown unless you dry it, set the pan over high heat, and don't crowd the meat in the pan.

MASTER RECIPE

Beef Bourguignon—Beef in Red Wine Sauce *Serves 6 to 8*

Cooking time: about 2½ hours.

Optional, but traditional for added flavor: 6 ounces blanched bacon *lardons* (see box, page 60)
2 to 3 Tbs cooking oil
About 4 pounds trimmed beef chuck, cut into 2-inch cubes
Salt and freshly ground pepper
2 cups sliced onions
1 cup sliced carrots
1 bottle red wine (such as zinfandel or Chianti)
2 cups beef stock (page 5) or canned beef broth
1 cup chopped tomatoes, fresh or canned
1 medium herb bouquet (see box, page 58)
Beurre manié for the sauce: 3 Tbs flour blended to a paste with 2 Tbs butter
For the garnish: 24 brown-braised small white onions (page 28) and 3 cups sautéed quartered mushrooms (page 31)

(If using *lardons*, sauté them to brown lightly in a little oil; set them aside and add to simmer with the beef, using the rendered fat in browning.) Choose a large frying pan and brown the chunks of meat on all sides in hot oil, season with salt and pepper, and turn them into a heavy casserole. Remove all but a little fat from the frying pan, add the sliced vegetables and brown them, and add to the meat. Deglaze the pan with wine, pouring it into the casserole along with enough stock almost to cover the meat. Stir in the tomatoes and add the herb bouquet. Bring to the simmer, cover, and simmer slowly, either on the stove or in a preheated 325°F oven, until the meat is tender—eat a little piece to check.

Drain through a colander set over a saucepan and return the meat to the casserole. Press juices out of the residue into the cooking liquid, then degrease and boil down the liquid to 3 cups. Off heat, whisk in the *beurre manié*, then simmer for 2 minutes as the sauce thickens lightly. Correct seasoning and pour over the meat, folding in the onions and mushrooms. (May be completed a day in advance to this point.)

To serve, bring to the simmer, basting meat and vegetables with the sauce for several minutes until thoroughly hot throughout.

BLANCHED BACON AND *LARDONS*. When you can't find a piece of pork fat to protect the surface of roasting meat, use sliced bacon or salt pork, but you need to remove its smoky or salty taste. To do so, drop 6 to 8 slices into 2 quarts of cold water, bring to the boil, and simmer 6 to 8 minutes. Drain, rinse in cold water, and dry on paper towels. *Lardons*, pieces of blanched bacon or salt pork cut into ¼-inch-thick pieces about 1 inch long, are used for flavoring dishes such as beef bourguignon and coq au vin.

VARIATIONS

■ **POT ROAST AND DAUBE OF BEEF.** For a 4-to-5-pound bottom round or top round of beef, serving 10 to 12. (Other possibilities: chuck shoulder, eye of round, middle cut of brisket.) Simmering time: 3 to 4 hours. Brown the beef on all sides, either on top of the stove or under the broiler, turning and basting with oil. Season with salt and pepper and set in a covered casserole with the same browned sliced vegetables, wine, stock, and other ingredients as for the preceding master recipe. When tender, proceed to make the sauce in the same manner.

■ **COQ AU VIN—CHICKEN IN RED WINE.** For 3 pounds of cut-up frying chicken, serving 5 or 6 people. Cooking time: 25 to 30 minutes. Brown the chicken all over in hot oil and the rendered fat from the optional *lardons*. Then proceed exactly as for the master beef recipe, using the same ingredients and the garniture of onions and mushrooms.

■ CHICKEN FRICASSEE. The fricassee is essentially the same as the coq au vin, but it is done in white wine rather than red, and the chicken is not browned. For 3 pounds of chicken, serving 5 to 6. Cooking time: 25 to 30 minutes. When 3 tablespoons of butter are foaming in the frying pan, stir in 1 cup of sliced onions; when they are tender, add the chicken pieces. Turn frequently until stiffened slightly but not browned. Season with salt and pepper, add a pinch of tarragon, cover, and cook very slowly for 5 minutes more, without coloring. Then simmer with 2 cups of dry white wine or $1\frac{1}{2}$ cups of dry French vermouth and about 2 cups of chicken broth. Complete the sauce as described in the master recipe and garnish with white-braised little onions (page 28) and simmered mushrooms (page 32). You may wish to enrich the sauce with a little cream.

Lamb Stew

(Note that this is always called a stew but it is actually a braise, because the meat is browned.) For 4 to 5 pounds bone-in lamb shoulder cut into 2-inch chunks, serving 6. Cooking time: about $1\frac{1}{2}$ hours. Brown the lamb and $1\frac{1}{2}$ cups sliced onions as in the master recipe. Season and turn into a casserole with 2 smashed cloves garlic, $\frac{1}{2}$ teaspoon rosemary, $1\frac{1}{2}$ cups dry white wine or dry white French vermouth, 1 cup chopped tomatoes, and enough chicken broth barely to cover ingredients. Simmer about $1\frac{1}{2}$ hours and finish the sauce as suggested in the master recipe.

Lamb Shanks

1 or 2 hind lamb shanks per person, or 1 foreshank sawed into 2-inch lengths. Prepare them exactly as for the preceding lamb stew.

Ossobuco

Veal hind shanks sawed into $1\frac{1}{2}$-to-2-inch lengths, 2 or 3 per person. Cooking time: about $1\frac{1}{2}$ hours. Season and dredge the meat in flour just before browning—because of the flour, the sauce will need no further thickening. Simmer with chicken stock (page 4), sliced sautéed onions, and dry white wine or dry French vermouth. Finish with a sprinkling of gremolata—finely minced zest of an orange and a lemon, a minced clove of garlic, and a handful of chopped parsley.

FISH AND SHELLFISH—
POACHING AND STEAMING

Fish Fillets Poached in White Wine

For sole, trout, and other thin skinless boneless fillets, 5 to 6 ounces per serving. Cooking time: about 10 minutes. For 6 fillets. Score the skin sides of the fish and season with salt and white pepper. Sprinkle 1 tablespoon of minced shallots in the bottom of a buttered baking dish; lay in the fillets, skin side down and lightly overlapping. Scatter another tablespoon of shallots on top. Pour around them ⅔ cup of dry white wine or dry white French vermouth, and ⅓ cup of fish stock, chicken stock, or water. Cover with buttered wax paper and bring just to the simmer on top of the stove, then set in a preheated 350°F oven. The fish is done in 7 to 8 minutes, when just lightly springy to the touch and opaque (milky white). Drain cooking juices into a saucepan and boil down rapidly until almost syrupy. For a simple sauce, whisk in droplets of lemon juice and minced parsley and, if you wish, a tablespoon or two of butter. Spoon over the fish and serve at once.

Sea Scallops Poached in White Wine

For 1½ pounds whole scallops, serving 6. Simmer ½ tablespoon minced shallots for 3 minutes with ⅓ cup each of dry white French vermouth and water plus ½ teaspoon salt and a small imported bay leaf. Then add the scallops and simmer 1½ to 2 minutes, just until lightly springy to the touch. Remove from heat and let cool in the liquid at least 10 minutes, to pick up its flavor. Remove scallops, discard bay leaf, and rapidly boil down liquid until almost syrupy.

NOTE: *Simmering times* for quartered sea scallops and bay scallops, 15 to 30 seconds; for calicos, bring just to the simmer.

SERVING SUGGESTIONS

■ **FINES HERBES.** Stir fresh minced parsley and/or dill, tarragon or chives into the reduced liquid, and briefly reheat scallops, folding in, if you wish, a few tablespoons of heavy cream.

■ **PROVENÇAL—WITH TOMATOES.** Stir 1½ cups peeled, seeded, juiced, and chopped fresh tomatoes (see box, page 30) and 1 large clove of minced garlic into the reduced liquid. Cover and simmer 5 minutes, then uncover and boil down rapidly to thicken. Season. Fold in the scallops and reheat briefly. Fold in minced parsley or other green herbs and serve.

Poached Salmon Fillets

For 8 salmon fillets 6 to 8 ounces each. Bring 2 quarts of water to the boil in a large skillet, adding 1 tablespoon salt and ¼ cup white-wine vinegar. Slide in the salmon, bring back almost to the simmer, and poach just below the simmer for 8 minutes—the fish is done when just springy to the touch. Drain, remove skin, and serve with lemon wedges, melted butter, or hollandaise sauce (page 13).

Whole Steamed Salmon

A 5-to-6-pound salmon serves 10 to 12. Cooking time: about 45 minutes. Have the salmon eviscerated, gills removed, and fins trimmed. Brush outside with oil and season cavity with salt and pepper. Lay the fish on an oiled rack in a fish poacher or roaster and wrap rack and salmon in washed cheesecloth. Strew around the fish 2 cups of thinly sliced sautéed onions and 1 cup each of sautéed sliced carrots and celery, and a medium herb bouquet with parsley, bay, and tarragon. Pour in 4 cups of dry white wine or 3 cups of dry white French vermouth plus fish or light chicken stock to a depth of 1 inch. Bring to the simmer on top of the stove and seal top of poacher with heavy foil and a lid. Maintain at a slow simmer, basting rapidly several times with pan liquids. The fish is done at a thermometer reading of 150°F. Remove fish, slide onto serving platter, and keep warm. Drain cooking liquid out of poacher into saucepan, pressing juices out of vegetables. Boil down to a syrupy 1 cup. Enrich, if you wish, with heavy cream and a swirling of butter and chopped fresh parsley.

Steamed Lobsters

Approximate cooking times: 10 minutes for 1-pounders; 12 to 13 for 1¼-pounders; 14 to 15 for 1½-pounders; 18 minutes for 2-pounders. Fit a rack in a 5-gallon pot and fill with 2 inches of seawater, or tap water with 1½ teaspoons salt per quart. Cover and bring to the rapid boil, then quickly drop in 6 live lobsters headfirst. Cover the pot and weight down the lid to make a firm seal. As soon as steam appears, begin timing as indicated. A lobster is probably done when the long antennas pull out easily. But to be sure, turn the lobster over and slit open the chest to see the tomalley—if all black, cook several minutes more, until tomalley is pale green. Accompany with melted butter and lemon wedges.

Egg Cookery

"It behooves us to choose eggs carefully and to treat them right."

Eggs appear throughout cookery not only as themselves—in their omelet, scrambled, poached, stuffed, and soft-boiled guises—but as puff producers in cakes and soufflés, as thickeners for sauces and custards, and, of course, as the stars and starters for those two noble and addictive creations, hollandaise and mayonnaise.

BUYING AND STORING EGGS. It behooves us to choose eggs carefully and to treat them right. Because at room temperature they make a warm and comfortable home for evil bacteria, always buy refrigerated eggs, never buy cracked or dirty eggs, always bring your eggs home in a refrigerated container, and keep eggs chilled until the moment you are to use them.

MASTER RECIPE

The French Omelet

The perfect omelet is a gently oval shape of coagulated egg enclosing a tender custard of eggs. It can be a plain breakfast omelet flavored only with salt, pepper, and butter, or it can be a quick main course luncheon omelet filled or garnished with chicken livers, mushrooms, spinach, truffles, smoked salmon, or whatever the cook wishes—an attractive use for nice leftovers, by the way. And you can make an omelet in a number of ways, such as the scrambled technique, the tilt-and-fold method, and so forth. I have always preferred the 2-to-3-egg omelet made by my old French chef teacher's shake-and-jerk system, as follows.

If this is your first attempt, go through the movements of the jerk—and note it is not a toss, it is a straight jerk toward you—and practice the unmolding technique. Serve the whole family for breakfast, so you'll be making 4 or 5 omelets or more and will get the feel. It's a very fast lesson, since an omelet takes only about 20 seconds to make.

For a 2-to-3-egg omelet, serving 1 person

2 jumbo or extra-large eggs, or 3 large or
    medium eggs
Big pinch of salt
Several grinds of pepper
1 tsp cold water, optional, for a more
    perfect blending of yolks and whites
1 Tbs unsalted butter

Have a warm plate at your side, as well as butter, a sprig or two of parsley, and a rubber spatula. Break the eggs into a mixing bowl and whisk just enough to blend them with the salt, pepper, and optional water.

Set the omelet pan (see box) over highest heat, add the butter, and tilt pan in all directions to film bottom and sides. When the butter foam has almost subsided but just before the butter browns, pour in the eggs. Shake the pan briefly by its handle to spread the eggs over the bottom of the pan. Hold still for several seconds while the eggs coagulate on the bottom. Then start jerking the pan toward you, throwing the egg mass against the far edge. Keep jerking roughly, gradually lifting up by the handle and tilting the far edge of the pan over the heat as the omelet begins to roll over on itself. Push any stray egg back into the mass with the rubber spatula, then bang on the handle close to the pan with your fist, and the omelet will start curling at its far edge.

To unmold, rapidly turn the pan handle to your right and grab its underside with your right hand, palm up under the handle and thumb on top. Holding the plate in your left hand, tilt pan and plate toward each other, turning the pan down over the plate, and the omelet falls into place. Push the sides neatly in place with the spatula if necessary.

Spear a lump of butter with a fork, rapidly brush a little of it over the top, decorate with a sprig of parsley, and serve.

THE OMELET PAN. To make omelets you must have a nonstick pan, and fortunately these are easily available. I highly recommend the professional nonstick aluminum shape with a long handle and sloping sides, 10 inches in top diameter and 7½ at the bottom. I use the Wearever aluminum, available in many hardware stores.

VARIATIONS

■ **FINES HERBES.** Mince chives and parsley, or tarragon, or chervil, whisk ½ tablespoon into the eggs as you make the omelet, and sprinkle a bit on top for serving.

■ **FILLED OMELETS.** You can either cut a split lengthwise in the finished omelet with a knife and spread on a heaping spoonful of filling, or you can spoon the filling onto the eggs in the pan, just as they coagulate enough to hold and before you start the final rolling—this takes a little special maneuvering but you will work out your own system.

Some Suggested Fillings and Garnishes

1- Creamed cooked chopped spinach (page 25), or cooked chopped broccoli (page 25), sautéed in butter

2- Quartered or sliced mushrooms, chicken livers, or scallops sautéed in butter with shallots and seasonings (cook as for the scallops, page 41)

3- Creamed lobster, shrimp, or crab (see box, page 66)

4- Pipérade—green and red peppers sautéed with onions, garlic, and herbs (page 32)

5- Potatoes—sautéed diced potatoes (page 36), to which you could add bacon and onions

6- Tomato—fresh tomato fondue (see box, page 30)

CREAMED LOBSTER, CRAB, OR SHRIMP. For about 1 cup, enough to fill or garnish 4 to 6 omelets. Briefly sauté 1 tablespoon finely minced shallots in 2 tablespoons butter until softened, then fold in 1 cup cooked shellfish meat cut into ¼-inch pieces. When well warmed through, season lightly with salt and pepper, and boil for a minute or two with 2 tablespoons dry white French vermouth, then briefly with ½ cup heavy cream, until nicely thickened. Correct seasoning, and, if you wish, fold in a sprinkling of minced fresh parsley.

Scrambled Eggs

We so often think of scrambled eggs served only with bacon or sausage for an everyday breakfast, but they make a fine fancy breakfast or even luncheon dish with baked tomatoes, sautéed potatoes, asparagus tips, and all manner of garnishes. Scrambled eggs are also good cold, as you will see later on, but I don't think these do well when mixed up with other things. I like them to stand alone and be garnished on the side.

For 8 eggs, serving 4 people. Scrambled eggs should be soft, broken curds, and the more gently and slowly you cook them, the more tender and delicious they will be. Choose the same 10-inch heavy nonstick pan used for the preceding omelets. Have warm but not hot plates at hand. Whisk the eggs in a mixing bowl just to blend whites and yolks, adding ¼ teaspoon salt (or to taste) and several grinds of pepper. Set the pan over moderate heat with 1 tablespoon unsalted butter, and when it is melted, swirl the pan to cover bottom and sides.

Pour all but 2 tablespoons of the eggs into the pan, turn heat to moderately low, and start slowly scraping the eggs from the bottom of the pan as they very gradually coagulate into soft curds. This will take several minutes. When they are thickened as you wish, remove pan from heat and, to stop the cooking and cream the eggs, fold in the remainder of the beaten egg. Taste, and correct seasoning. If you wish, fold in a tablespoon or so of soft unsalted butter or of heavy cream. Serve at once.

ADDITIONS AND VARIATIONS

■ SUGGESTED ACCOMPANIMENTS *(other than crisp bacon, ham, sausages, and so forth)*

1- Buttered toast points—neat, small triangles of white toast

2- Tomatoes Provençal—tomato halves baked with seasoned bread crumbs (page 29)

3- Cooked asparagus tips warmed in butter

4- Any of the garnishes suggested for the omelets (page 65)

■ COLD SCRAMBLED EGGS IN A TOMATO SHELL. Fold pipérade (page 32) into the just-scrambled eggs. Season well, mound into hollowed-out halves of fresh ripe tomatoes, and chill.

■ COLD SCRAMBLED EGGS WITH DILL. Season the just-scrambled eggs with chopped fresh dill, chill, and serve with smoked salmon.

Poached Eggs

The versatile poached egg! Serve it hot in an artichoke cup, or crowned with béarnaise atop a tenderloin steak, or glittering in aspic, or gracing a curly endive salad, or buried in a soufflé, or dressed as a Benedict, or simply sitting on a warm, crisp, buttery piece of toast for breakfast. It's a graceful oval, whose white is softly set and whose yolk is thickly liquid. If we could have them fresh from the hen they would literally poach by themselves, since a really fresh egg holds its shape when dropped into simmering water. But most of us have to take certain steps to assure success, using either vinegared water or oval metal egg-poachers (which you can buy in some cookware shops).

To Help the Egg Keep Its Shape. Using a pushpin, pierce a hole ¼ inch deep in the large end of the egg to release the air pocket (otherwise the egg will crack). To help the egg keep its shape, lower not more than 4 eggs at a time into a pan of rapidly boiling water. Boil for exactly 10 seconds, then remove with a slotted spoon.

Vinegared Water. To poach up to 6 eggs, bring 1½ quarts of water and ¼ cup white vinegar (which helps the white to coagulate) to the simmer in a saucepan 8 inches in diameter and 3 inches deep. Have a kitchen timer and slotted spoon at hand. One by one, starting near the pan handle and moving clockwise, hold the egg as close to the surface as possible, and break it into the water. Rapidly continue with the rest. Maintain the water at the simmer and poach exactly 4 minutes—the white should be softly set and the yolk liquid. Clockwise from the handle of the pan, remove the eggs one by one with the perforated spoon, and drop into a basin of cold water to wash off the vinegar.

Poaching in the Perforated Oval Metal Container. Set the poachers in a pan of simmering water to cover, drop in the pierced, 10-second-boiled eggs, and poach at the simmer for exactly 4 minutes, as described above. Remove the poachers and dislodge the eggs carefully with a soup spoon.

Eggs May Be Poached a Day or Two in Advance. Submerge in fresh cold water and refrigerate uncovered.

To Serve Cold. Store as above, or chill for 10 minutes in ice water. Remove one by one with a slotted spoon, and roll over a clean towel to blot off water.

To Serve Hot. Lower chilled eggs into a pan of lightly salted simmering water and let warm up for 1 minute, then remove.

VARIATIONS

▮ EGGS BENEDICT. Toast and butter English-muffin halves or crustless circles of brioche bread (which I prefer, since I find the muffins tough and hard to cut). Top each toast with a round of sautéed ham, a warm poached egg, and hollandaise sauce (page 13). Then, if you are feeling luxurious, slide on a warm, buttery slice of black truffle.

▮ SOUFFLÉ VENDÔME. Arrange 4 toasted and buttered French-bread rounds (see box, page 7) in a 6-cup baking dish, and top with 4 cold poached eggs. Cover with the cheese soufflé on page 71, and bake as directed. This dish always amazes your guests, and the eggs emerge perfectly done.

▮ SALAD OF CURLY ENDIVE WITH BACON AND POACHED EGGS. See page 18.

Shirred Eggs

Here, for individual servings, the egg or eggs are broken into a shallow dish and started on top of the stove but finished under the broiler. The white is softly set but the yolk is filmed over with a translucent film. A deliciously buttery egg dish, but hardly a diet one!

Here is how to proceed. Provide yourself with a sufficient number of shallow flameproof baking dishes about 4 inches across, slide the oven rack onto the upper level, preheat the broiler, and melt about 2 tablespoons butter per serving. For each serving, set one of the dishes over moderately low heat and pour in 1 tablespoon melted butter. When bubbling, break in 1 or 2 eggs and cook for about 30 seconds, just to set a thin layer of white in the bottom of the dish. Remove from heat, and baste top of eggs with a teaspoon of melted butter. Place on a baking sheet, and do the same with your other baking dishes. Just before serving, set 1 inch under the broiler and cook for about 1 minute, sliding dishes in and out every few seconds and basting with a little more butter. When the whites are set and the yolks are filmed, season and serve immediately.

ADDITIONS AND VARIATIONS

▮ SHIRRED EGGS WITH CREAM. After starting the eggs on top of the stove, pour 2 tablespoons of heavy cream over

Top:
Forming a round loaf

Bottom:
Beating egg whites to stiff,
shining peaks

Goose ready to take off

A long-handled brush is handy for basting a turkey.

Top: Smoothing melted chocolate
Bottom: Proudly showing a finished cake

them and set under the broiler to finish. No basting is necessary.

■ SHIRRED EGGS GRATINÉED WITH CHEESE. Proceed as with the cream, above, topping it with a teaspoon of grated Swiss or Parmesan cheese.

■ SHIRRED EGGS *AU BEURRE NOIR*— WITH BLACK BUTTER SAUCE. Use just a teaspoon of butter to baste the eggs under the broiler, and when done, dress them with black-butter sauce (see box), adding the suggested chopped parsley and capers as well.

■ GARNITURES. Just before serving, you could surround the eggs with sautéed mushrooms, kidneys, chicken livers, tomato sauce, sautéed green and red peppers, or whatever. However, I think the following eggs in ramekins take better to such additions.

BLACK BUTTER SAUCE—*BEURRE NOIR.* A wonderful sauce for fish and egg dishes. For about ½ cup, cut 1 stick of butter into ¼-inch slices and melt in a 6-inch frying pan. When bubbling, increase heat to high. Swirl the pan by its handle as the bubbles subside and the butter rapidly begins to brown. In a few seconds, as soon as it is a nice walnut brown (not black!), pour it over the food.

NOTE: Before saucing the food, you may wish to sprinkle on a teaspoon or so of chopped fresh parsley, which will sizzle as the hot sauce goes over it, then swirl a tablespoon or so of capers in the pan, and divide them over the sauced food.

Eggs Baked in Ramekins

These are a more leisurely egg dish than the preceding shirred eggs, with their rapid ins and outs from under the broiler. Here the eggs are broken into little buttered custard cups, and set in a pan of hot water to bake in the oven for 7 to 10 minutes. They can be simple, with just a base of cream, or you can put a filling in the bottom of the cup—a great way to use leftover cooked spinach, chopped mushrooms, cooked onions, or whatever enticing item you have on hand.

Slide the rack onto the lower-middle level, and preheat the oven to 375°F. For each serving, pour 1 tablespoon heavy cream into a buttered ½-cup ramekin and place in a pan containing ½ inch of simmering water over moderate heat. When the cream is hot, break in 1 or 2 eggs; pour over another tablespoon of cream; and top with a dot of butter. Bake for 7 to 10 minutes, until softly set—they should still tremble slightly, since they will set a little more in their ramekins after being removed from the oven. Remove from the oven; season with salt and pepper, and serve.

ADDITIONS AND VARIATIONS

■ AUX FINES HERBES—WITH MINCED GREEN HERBS. Add a teaspoon or so to the cream for each serving—

one or a mixture of parsley, chives, tarragon, chervil.

▉ WITH VARIOUS SAUCES. Instead of cream, use a brown sauce with mushrooms, a cheese sauce, a tomato sauce, a curry sauce, an onion sauce, etc. A good occasion for using up your precious leftovers.

▉ BOTTOM FILLERS. Spread in the bottom of each ramekin a tablespoon or so of such attractive items as cooked and nicely flavored diced asparagus, broccoli, spinach, artichoke bottoms, diced ham, mushrooms, chicken livers, or shellfish. A slice of black truffle would be a happy surprise, as would a generous spoonful of foie gras.

Hard-Boiled Eggs

When you are stuffing hard-boiled eggs for the family, it is just too bad if they refuse to peel neatly, but when you are doing them for a party, it's a disaster. The following rather cumbersome system, developed by the State of Georgia Egg Board, pretty well solves the problem.

For 12 eggs (I don't recommend more at one time). Pierce a pinhole ¼ inch deep into the large end of each egg—allowing the air bubble to escape. Place the eggs in a deep saucepan and cover with 3½ quarts of cold water. Bring just to the rolling boil, remove from heat, cover the pan, and let sit for exactly 17 minutes. Transfer the eggs to a bowl of ice and water and let chill for 2 minutes—to shrink the egg body from the shell. Meanwhile, reheat cooking water to the boil. Lower 6 chilled eggs at a time into the boiling water and let boil exactly 10 seconds—to expand the shell from the egg body.

Let chill for 20 minutes or more— well-chilled eggs are easier to peel. To peel, crack each egg gently all over on your work surface, then peel under a small stream of cold water, starting at the large end. The eggs will keep perfectly for several days when submerged in cold water and left uncovered in the refrigerator.

VARIATIONS

▉ A SIMPLE BASE FOR COLD STUFFED EGGS. For 2 dozen egg halves. Slice 12 peeled chilled eggs in half lengthwise, and sieve the yolks into a bowl. Blend in 2 tablespoons each of mayonnaise and softened unsalted butter, and season to taste with salt and freshly ground white pepper. Pipe the stuffing into the egg-white halves using a pastry bag fitted with a star tip. Decorate, if you wish, with parsley sprigs and bits of red pimiento. Or finely mince and add to the base stuffing any of the following:

1- Fresh green herbs such as dill, basil, tarragon, parsley, chives, chervil

2- Cooked asparagus tips

3- Minced onions sautéed in butter with a pinch of curry powder

4- Sautéed mushroom duxelles (page 32)

5- Lobster, crab, or shrimp sautéed in butter and seasonings (see box, page 66)

6- Smoked salmon

7- Pickles—sweet relish or dills

8- Black-olive *tapénade* (see box)

TAPÉNADE. 1 cup pitted Mediterranean-style black olives, 3 tablespoons capers, 6 oil-packed anchovy fillets, and 1 large clove of puréed garlic all ground to a paste in a food processor.

■ BAKED STUFFED EGGS. A very French luncheon or supper dish. Sieve the yolks and blend in heavy cream and a stuffing, such as minced mushrooms.

Stuffed Eggs au Gratin, Chimay. For 4 people. Sieve the yolks of a dozen hard-boiled eggs and blend in 1/4 cup or so each of heavy cream and mushroom duxelles (page 32). Bake them, 6 halves at a time, in individual dishes, in a well-seasoned cheese sauce, exactly as for the cauliflower au gratin on page 31.

SOUFFLÉS

The soufflé is the egg at its most magnificent. How glorious it is when borne to the table, its head rising dramatically out of its dish, and swaying voluptuously as it is set down. Invite special guests to lunch and you couldn't serve them a more appropriate and attractive light meal than cheese soufflé and a green salad, or plan on a chocolate soufflé as a loving treat for your most favorite dinner guests. Fortunately, a reasonably well-assembled soufflé is an automatic happening. It is simply a flavored sauce base into which you fold stiffly beaten egg whites, and depends almost entirely on how you beat your egg whites and how you fold them in—and these two specifics are fully explained in the cake section on pages 100 and 98.

MASTER RECIPE

Savory Cheese Soufflé *For a 4-to-6-cup soufflé mold or straight-sided baking dish 8 inches across, serving 4*

You can bake this in a 4-cup mold with a paper collar, into which the soufflé will puff 2 to 3 inches over the rim and hold its puff when the collar is removed. Or

bake it in a 6-cup mold, which will give you a more stable soufflé but less puff.

1 to 1½ Tbs soft butter for the soufflé dish and collar
2 Tbs finely grated Parmesan cheese for the soufflé dish
2½ Tbs butter for the soufflé
3 Tbs flour
1 cup hot milk

¼ tsp paprika
A speck of grated nutmeg
½ tsp salt
2 or 3 grinds of white pepper
4 egg yolks
5 egg whites
1 cup (3½ ounces) coarsely grated
 Swiss cheese

Prepare the soufflé dish. (See box at right.) Slide rack onto lower-third level, and preheat oven to 400°F.

The Sauce Base. Cook the 2½ tablespoons butter and 3 tablespoons flour together in a 3-quart saucepan until they foam and froth for 2 minutes. Remove from heat and beat in the hot milk, then simmer and stir slowly for a minute or two to thicken. Remove from heat and whisk seasonings into sauce, then, one by one, the egg yolks.

Whip the egg whites to stiff, shining peaks (see box, page 100). Whisk a quarter of them into the sauce to lighten it, then delicately fold in the rest of the whites, alternating with sprinklings of the grated Swiss cheese.

Turn the soufflé mixture into the dish and set in the oven. Reduce heat to 375°F and bake 25 to 30 minutes, until soufflé has puffed several inches into the collar, or an inch or two above the rim, and has browned nicely on top. When is it really done? See box on page 73.

Remove the collar and serve at once.

To Serve a Soufflé. So as to deflate it as little as possible, hold a serving spoon and fork upright and back to back. Plunge them into the center of the soufflé and tear it apart.

TO PREPARE THE SOUFFLÉ DISH. Choose a straight-sided baking dish or a "charlotte" mold. Smear a light coating of soft butter over the insides of the dish, covering bottom and sides. Depending on the soufflé, roll finely grated Parmesan cheese, or bread crumbs, or granulated sugar in the dish to cover inner surface completely, and knock out excess.

The Collar. If you are using a collar, cut a length of parchment paper or aluminum foil long enough to wrap around the dish with a 2-inch overlap, fold in half lengthwise, and butter one side. Wrap the collar around the dish, buttered side in; it should rise 3 inches above the rim. Secure in place with 2 straight pins, inserted heads up for quick removal.

VARIATIONS

▥ **VEGETABLE SOUFFLÉS.** After making the sauce base, fold in ¼ to ⅓ cup of well-seasoned cooked chopped spinach, asparagus, broccoli, or mushrooms. Complete the soufflé as directed, but fold in only ⅓ cup of the grated Swiss cheese.

▥ **SHELLFISH SOUFFLÉS.** Make a cup or so of creamed lobster, crab or shrimp (see box, page 66) and spread in the bottom of the buttered soufflé dish.

Cover with the soufflé mixture but fold in only ⅓ cup of the grated Swiss cheese. You might serve the fresh tomato fondue (see box, page 30) along with it.

■ SALMON AND OTHER FISH IN SOUFFLÉS. The soufflé is a dressy solution for leftover fish. Stir a cup or so of cooked flaked fish into the sauce base, and give extra flavor by adding several tablespoons of minced shallots sautéed in butter and a tablespoon or two of minced fresh dill. Again, cut down the grated Swiss cheese to ⅓ cup. Hollandaise sauce (page 13) would go well here.

WHEN IS THE SOUFFLÉ DONE? If it has a collar, rapidly release it just a bit to check—if the puff sags, refasten the collar and bake a few minutes more. When a skewer is plunged down into the side of the puff and comes out with a few particles clinging, the soufflé will be deliciously creamy inside but will not hold up long. If the skewer comes out clean, it will hold up a little longer.

■ SOUFFLÉ ON A PLATTER. Rather than in a deep dish, you may bake a soufflé on a platter or in a gratin dish. For 4 people, butter a 12-to-14-inch oval ovenproof platter and arrange on it four ½-cup mounds of a deliciously flavored something, like the creamed shellfish on page 66. Heap a quarter of the finished soufflé mixture over each, top with grated Swiss cheese, and bake 15 minutes or so in a preheated 425°F oven, until puffed and brown.

■ SOUFFLÉ ROULADE—THE ROLLED SOUFFLÉ. For an 11-by-17-inch jelly-roll pan, serving 6 to 8 people. Slide rack onto upper-third level of oven, and preheat to 425°F. Butter the pan and line with parchment or wax paper, leaving a 2-inch overhang at each end. Butter the paper and flour it, knocking out excess. Follow the master recipe, but increase proportions to the following: 5 tablespoons butter, 6 tablespoons flour, 1½ cups milk, 6 yolks, 7 whites, and 1 cup of grated Swiss cheese. Spread the soufflé mixture in the pan and bake for 12 minutes or so, until just well set—don't overcook, or it will crack when rolled. Sprinkle bread crumbs over the top and invert the soufflé onto another paper-covered baking sheet. Carefully peel off the paper lining. Spread over the soufflé 1¼ cups or so of any warm, well-seasoned filling, such as pipérade (page 32), sautéed mushrooms and diced ham, the creamed shellfish on page 66, or other. Roll up the soufflé and top decoratively, if you wish, with more filling, and/or a sauce such as the tomato fondue on page 30, or hollandaise, page 13.

DESSERT SOUFFLÉS

Soufflé for dessert—that always means a party. The same general principles of the beating and folding in of egg whites apply to sweet soufflés as to main-course soufflés, but since dessert soufflés should be light and airy, there are differences in the sauce base. You could use a white sauce or a pastry cream, but I prefer the *bouillie,* outlined below, and you'll note that the egg whites are given more body by being beaten with sugar.

MASTER RECIPE

Vanilla Soufflé *For a 6-cup soufflé dish, serving 4 people*

3 Tbs flour
¼ cup milk
⅓ cup plus 2 Tbs granulated sugar
4 egg yolks
2 Tbs butter, softened (optional)
5 egg whites
2 Tbs pure vanilla extract
Confectioners' sugar in a fine sieve

Prepare the soufflé dish and affix the paper collar as directed in the box on page 72. Slide the rack onto the lower-third level of the oven, and preheat to 400°F.

Whisk the flour and half the milk in a saucepan. When well blended, whisk in the remaining milk and the ⅓ cup sugar. Then bring to the boil and boil slowly, whisking, for 30 seconds. This is now a *bouillie.* Remove from heat; let cool for a moment, then, one by one, beat in the yolks and the optional butter.

Whip the egg whites to soft peaks, sprinkle in the 2 tablespoons sugar, and beat to stiff, shining peaks (see box, page 100). Whisk the vanilla into the sauce base, then whisk in a quarter of the whites to lighten it. Delicately fold in remaining whites and turn the mixture into the prepared dish.

Set in the oven, reduce heat to 375°F, and bake until the soufflé has begun to puff and brown—about 20 minutes. Rapidly slide out rack, and dust the top of the soufflé with confectioners' sugar. Continue baking until it has puffed high into the collar. When is it done? See box on page 73.

Remove collar and serve at once.

VARIATIONS

■ ORANGE SOUFFLÉ GRAND MARNIER. Follow the master recipe above, but purée the zest (colored part of peel) of a large orange with the ⅓ cup sugar in a blender or food processor, and use in the sauce base. Stir only 2 teaspoons vanilla into the base, but add 3 tablespoons orange liqueur.

■ CHOCOLATE SOUFFLÉ. Follow the preceding master recipe, but prepare a 2-quart dish to serve 8. Preheat oven to

425°F. Melt 7 ounces semisweet chocolate with ⅓ cup strong coffee (see box, page 103). Make sauce base as directed in master recipe, using ⅓ cup flour and 2 cups milk; whisk at the slow boil for 2 minutes. Off heat, beat in 3 tablespoons optional butter, 1 tablespoon vanilla extract, a big pinch of salt, 4 egg yolks, and the melted chocolate. Whip 6 egg whites to soft peaks, add ½ cup sugar and whip to shiny peaks (see box, page 100). Combine by ladling chocolate base down sides of egg-white bowl and folding rapidly to combine. Turn mixture into dish, set into oven, reduce to 375°F, and bake for 40 minutes, or until puff starts. Dust with confectioners' sugar and bake until done (see box, page 73). Serve with lightly whipped *crème Chantilly* (page 101).

SAVORY CUSTARDS

We often think of custards only as desserts—particularly everybody's favorite, caramel custard (I'd like to be spooning up one of those right now!). But custards can also be main-course luncheon or supper dishes, or can accompany roasts, broils, and steaks. Whenever you are thinking of a soufflé on the menu, think also of its alternative, the custard—or timbale, in fancy-food language. It's easier to make, and you need have no qualms about the perfection of your egg whites or about collapses. The custard holds, it waits, it can be rewarmed, it's a smooth and sensuous pleasure to eat.

MASTER RECIPE

Individual Broccoli Timbales— Molded Custards *For 6 to 8 servings in 5-to-6-ounce (⅔-to-¾-cup) molds*

1½ to 2 Tbs softened butter (for the molds)
4 "large" eggs
2 cups cooked, chopped, well-seasoned broccoli florets (page 25)
2 Tbs grated onion
½ cup fresh white bread crumbs (see box, page 46)
2 to 3 Tbs minced fresh parsley

½ cup (2 ounces) lightly pressed down grated Swiss, cheddar, and/or mozzarella cheese
½ cup cream or milk
½ tsp salt
Several grinds of white pepper
Drops of Tabasco, optional

Smear softened butter inside the molds, slide rack onto lower-third level of oven, and preheat to 350°F. Provide yourself with a roasting pan to hold the molds, and have a kettle of boiling water ready.

Whisk the eggs in a mixing bowl to blend yolks and whites, then fold in all the remaining ingredients. Taste carefully, and correct seasoning. Ladle the mixture into the molds, filling them by about two-thirds.

Arrange the molds in the roasting pan and set in the oven. Pull the rack out, and pour in enough boiling water to come halfway up the sides of the molds. Very gently push the rack in, and bake 5 minutes, then lower heat to 325°F and bake about 25 minutes more. Adjust oven heat so that water in pan is never boiling, just almost bubbling.

When Are They Done? When a skewer plunged into the center comes out clean.

Carefully slide the roasting pan out of the oven and let the molds settle for 10 minutes—or a little longer, if need be.

To unmold, one by one run a sharp, thin knife around the inside of each mold and reverse it, dropping the custard onto a warm plate.

Serving Suggestions. Top with a sprinkling of toasted and buttered bread crumbs, or a tomato sauce (see box, page 30), or a béchamel sauce (page 13) enriched with chopped fresh herbs.

VARIATIONS

▦ **A LARGE TIMBALE.** Butter a 4-to-5-cup soufflé mold or high-sided baking dish and fill with the custard. Set in a roasting pan and pour in boiling water to come halfway up its sides. Bake as directed above.

▦ **FRESH CORN TIMBALE—CORN PUDDING.** Follow the master recipe, but substitute 2 cups of fresh corn scraped off the cob (8 to 10 ears), and 1 tablespoon of chopped fresh parsley.

▦ **OTHER VARIATIONS.** Cooked chopped spinach, asparagus tips, mushrooms, green and red peppers, shellfish, ham—any of these and more that you will think of can be substituted for the broccoli in the custard. It's a versatile formula.

MOLDED DESSERT CUSTARDS

MASTER RECIPE

Caramel Custard *For a 2-quart straight-sided baking dish, serving 8 to 10*

1 cup sugar and ⅓ cup water, for the caramel

6 "large" eggs
5 egg yolks
¾ cup sugar
1 quart hot milk
1 Tbs pure vanilla extract
Pinch of salt

Slide rack onto lower-middle level, and preheat the oven to 350°F. Cook the sugar and water to the caramel stage (see box, page 101), and pour half of it into the baking dish, swirling it rapidly around to coat bottom and sides. Add 4 to 5 tablespoons water to the remaining caramel in the pan and let simmer slowly to melt the caramel, thus turning it into a sauce for later.

Stir with a whisk (but do not beat and cause bubbles) the eggs, yolks, and sugar in a bowl to blend them. Then, a little at a time at first to dissolve the sugar, stir in the hot milk, then the vanilla and salt. Strain through a fine-meshed sieve into the caramelized dish. Set dish in a high-sided roasting pan on the oven rack, and pour in enough boiling water to come halfway up the outside of the dish.

Bake for about an hour, checking after 15 minutes to be sure water in roasting pan is maintained precisely at almost the simmer—little bubbles. If the water is too hot the custard will be grainy, but if not hot enough it will take hours to cook.

When Is It Done? When the center still trembles slightly, but a skewer plunged in 1 inch from the edge comes out clean.

Remove dish from roasting pan and let custard settle at least 30 minutes. The custard may be served warm, at room temperature, or chilled—if to be chilled, refrigerate, and cover when cold. (It can be refrigerated for 2 days.)

To Unmold. Run a thin-bladed knife between custard and edge of dish. Turn a serving plate upside down over the dish and reverse the two—the custard will slowly slip out. Pour the reserved caramel sauce around the custard.

VARIATIONS

▮ INDIVIDUAL CARAMEL CUSTARDS. The preceding proportions will fill a dozen 2/3-cup Pyrex bowls 3½ inches across. Line the bowls with caramel as described, fill with the custard mixture, and bake in a water bath at 350°F for 20 to 25 minutes, until set at the edges but with a slight tremble at the center. Unmold for serving.

▮ INDIVIDUAL MACAROON CUSTARDS. Caramelize individual bowls, as described above, and when hardened, smear with butter. Sprinkle pulverized macaroons in them to cover bottom and sides. Fill with the custard mixture. Bake, and unmold as described.

CUSTARD DESSERT SAUCES AND FILLINGS

Custard sauces are certainly essential to any cook's repertoire, the most important and useful being the classic *crème anglaise,* which is the basis for many desserts, ice creams, puddings, and other sauces. As with hollandaise, you have to deal with the egg yolk and its vagaries, but just remember that you are in control, and it is only the heat source that needs your full attention.

MASTER RECIPE

Crème Anglaise—Classic Custard Sauce *For about 2 cups*

6 egg yolks
½ cup sugar
1½ cups hot milk
3 Tbs butter, optional
1 Tbs pure vanilla extract
2 Tbs dark rum, cognac,
    or other liqueur, optional

Whisk the egg yolks in a 2-quart stainless-steel saucepan, adding the sugar by spoonfuls. Continue whisking for 2 to 3 minutes, until the yolks are thick and pale yellow and "form the ribbon" (see box, page 100). By dribbles at first, stir in the hot milk.

Set over moderate heat, stirring slowly and continuously with a wooden spoon, reaching all over the bottom of the pan as the custard gradually heats and thickens—do not let it come near the boil. If it seems to be getting too hot, lift pan up, then continue as the sauce

thickens. You are almost there when surface bubbles begin to disappear and you may see a whiff of steam arise.

When Is It Done? It coats the spoon in a light, creamy layer.

Beat in the optional butter, the vanilla, and the optional spirits. Serve warm, at room temperature, or chilled.

Storage. Remember that this is an egg-yolk sauce, and should not sit around at room temperature for more than ½ hour. To store for 2 to 3 days, refrigerate, and cover when cold.

Floating Island

A dramatic use for *crème anglaise*— huge caramel-streaked baked meringue chunks floating on a sea of custard sauce. For 6 to 8 servings, butter a 4-quart straight-sided baking dish and dust with confectioners' sugar. Set rack in lower-middle level of oven and preheat to 250°F.

Beat ⅔ cup egg whites (about 12) into soft peaks (see box, page 100), and continue beating to stiff, shining peaks while adding 1½ cups sugar by big spoonfuls. Turn this meringue into the baking dish. Bake 30 to 40 minutes, until the meringue has risen 3 to 4 inches and a skewer plunged down into the center comes out clean. Remove from oven and let cool—it will sink down. (May be baked several days in advance; may be frozen.)

To serve, pour 2 cups of *crème anglaise* (see preceding recipe) into a round serving dish. Unmold the meringue onto a baking sheet, cut into 6 to 8 big chunks, and arrange over the sauce. Boil 1 cup of sugar and ⅓ cup water to the caramel stage (see box, page 101), and when cooled slightly into a heavy syrup, weave decorative strands of caramel over the meringue, using the tines of a fork.

Pastry Cream—*Crème Pâtissière*

Custard filling for pies, tarts, cakes, and miscellaneous desserts. For about 2½ cups. Whisk 6 egg yolks in a stainless-steel saucepan, gradually adding ½ cup sugar and a pinch of salt. Continue until eggs are thick and pale yellow, and "form the ribbon" (see box, page 100). Sift on and whisk in ½ cup flour or cornstarch. By dribbles at first, whisk in 2 cups hot milk or half-and-half. Whisking slowly, bring to the boil, then whisk vigorously for a few seconds to smooth out any lumps. Simmer slowly, stirring with a wooden spoon, for 2 minutes, to cook the flour or starch. Remove from heat and blend in 1 tablespoon pure vanilla extract and, if you wish, 2 tablespoons each unsalted butter and rum or kirsch. Strain through a fine-meshed sieve into a bowl. Let cool, stirring up occasionally to prevent lumps.

To Store. Press a sheet of plastic wrap onto the surface to prevent a skin from forming; cover, and refrigerate for 2 to 3 days or freeze.

VARIATIONS AND ADDITIONS

▌TO LIGHTEN THE SAUCE, fold in ½ cup of whipped cream. Or give it volume and staying power by combining it with 2 cups of Italian meringue (page 102); just fold them together and you have created *crème Chiboust,* which you can then use as a cake filling or frosting, or as the custard base for fruit tarts.

Sabayon

A wine-custard sauce for fruit desserts. Whisk 1 egg, 2 egg yolks, ½ cup sugar, a pinch of salt, ⅓ cup Marsala, sherry, rum, or bourbon, and ⅓ cup dry white French vermouth in a stainless-steel saucepan. When well blended, whisk rather slowly over moderately low heat for 4 to 5 minutes, until sauce has thickened and is foamy, and quite warm to your finger—but do not let it come to the simmer. Serve warm or cold.

Classic Chocolate Mousse

Chocolate mousses were of this general type before the popularity of chocolate ganache (page 102), and the ganache is far quicker and easier, being only melted chocolate and heavy cream. You can make a ganache even more attractive when you fold in beaten egg whites, and you go to even greater heights when you blend in Italian meringue (page 102). However, the following smooth, rich, velvety classic continues to be my favorite of all chocolate mousses.

For about 5 cups, serving 6 to 8. Melt 6 ounces semisweet chocolate (see box, page 103) in 4 tablespoons strong coffee, and cut 1½ sticks of unsalted butter into rough slices, so it will soften. Meanwhile, beat together in a bowl 4 egg yolks and ¼ cup orange liqueur, gradually adding ¾ cup sugar, and continue beating until it is thick and pale yellow and "forms the ribbon" (see box, page 100). Set the bowl over a saucepan of barely simmering water and continue beating 4 to 5 minutes, until it is foamy, and warm to your finger. Remove from heat and beat over a bowl of cold water (or in a standing mixer) until it is cool and thick and again forms the ribbon.

When the chocolate has melted, smoothly blend in the butter, and fold into the egg-yolk mixture. Beat 4 egg whites to soft peaks, then to stiff, shining peaks with 2 tablespoons sugar (see box, page 100). Stir a quarter of this into the yolks and chocolate, then delicately fold in the rest.

Turn the mousse into a 6-cup serving dish or individual cups or *pots de crème*. Cover and chill for several hours (the mousse will keep in the refrigerator several days). Serve with lightly whipped cream (see box, page 101) or the above *crème anglaise*.

Breads, Crêpes, and Tarts

*"Of course you can buy a ready-made pie shell,
but it's a shame not to have the know-how yourself."*

BREADS

Yeast bread is a vast subject, comprising not only white bread and French bread but croissants, brioches, pumpernickel, whole wheat and rye, sourdoughs, and so forth. In this little book, therefore, I am concentrating only on some of the basics that apply to all of them.

Basic Dough for White Bread, French Breads, Pizzas, and Hard Rolls
Enough for one 2-quart loaf pan, 2 long fat French loaves, three 18-inch baguettes, two 9-inch round loaves, two 16-inch pizzas, or 12 rolls

1 package (a scant Tbs) active dry yeast
⅓ cup tepid water (not over 110°F)
Pinch of sugar
1 cup cold water, plus more if needed
3½ cups (1 pound) unbleached white all-purpose or bread flour, plus a little more if needed
1 Tbs rye or whole-wheat flour
2¼ tsp salt

Proof yeast in tepid water with the sugar for 5 minutes (see box), then stir in the cold water. Measure the flours and salt into the food processor fitted with a steel blade. With the machine running, rather slowly process in the yeast and water, adding driblets more cold water if needed, until the dough balls up on top of the blade. Let it revolve 8 to 10 times, then stop the machine and feel the dough. It should be reasonably soft and pliable. If damp and wet, process in a tablespoon or so more flour; if dry, add a dribble more cold water. Let rest for 5 minutes.

TO PROOF YEAST. It's always wise to make sure your yeast is really active. Stir a tablespoon of active dry yeast in a cup with 3 tablespoons of tepid water and a pinch of sugar. In 5 minutes it should begin to bubble. It's alive!

Process the dough another 15 seconds or so, then remove it to a floured board and let it rest 2 minutes. Knead it vigorously by hand a good 50 times, as described in the box below.

FINAL KNEADING OF DOUGH BY HAND. If you overknead in the processor, the dough can heat up; in addition, the gluten strands can break down, preventing a full rise. To finish the dough, fold it over on itself, then, with the heels of your hands, push it out in front of you, roughly, rapidly, and vigorously. Repeat about 50 times, until it is smooth and elastic and when you stretch the dough it holds together. It should not stick to your hands unless you pinch and hold a piece.

Preliminary Rise. Turn the dough into a 4-quart fairly straight-sided ungreased bowl. Cover bowl with plastic wrap and a towel, and set in a draft-free place—75°F is ideal. Dough will rise to 1½ times its original volume, usually in about 1 hour.

RESTING THE DOUGH. Flour contains both starch and gluten. The gluten holds the particles together and also allows the dough to hold its rise. However, gluten develops increasing resistance as the dough is worked, and it then becomes more and more difficult to manipulate. Whenever your dough won't roll easily, simply stop where you are and let it rest 10 minutes or so. The gluten will relax, and you can continue.

Second Rise. Turn dough out onto a lightly floured board. Push and pat it into a 14-inch rectangle and fold it into 3, like a business letter. Repeat a second time, then return it to the ungreased bowl, cover, and let rise again. It will rise to 2½ to 3 times its original volume, usually in 1 to 1½ hours. When almost tripled, the dough is ready to form and bake.

TEMPERATURES FOR RISING. Ideal temperatures are 70° to 75°F. Warmer, the rise is too fast and you miss out on flavor development. Colder is fine, even down to a refrigerator chill— you get flavor development—but it simply takes the dough longer to rise: the colder the environment, the longer it takes.

To Form and Bake 2 Long French Loaves

The very special movements here are designed to force the dough to develop a gluten cloak that holds as it bakes free-form into its characteristic loaf. Keep your work surface lightly floured at all times, so the gradually forming cloak will not tear. Set a smooth, lightly floured cotton or linen towel on a large rimless (or upside-down) baking sheet, to hold the formed loaves.

Cut the dough in half, then fold each piece in half. Cover one; push and pat the other into an 8-by-10-inch roughly rectangular shape.

Fold in half lengthwise. Press and pound firmly with your fist to seal the edges and flatten the dough to about its original shape.

Roll the dough so the seam is centered on top, and firmly press a rough trench into the seam with the side of your hand.

Using the seam as a guide, fold the dough in half lengthwise, and again press long edges together firmly to seal.

Starting at its center, begin rolling this length of dough under your open palms, gradually moving your hands apart and stretching the dough as you roll. Elongate the dough to about 18 inches (no longer than the length of your baking surface!) and place it seam side up on the long half of the lightly floured towel. I now like to pinch the sealed long edges securely together, just to be sure. Cover loosely with another floured towel while you form the second loaf the same way. Make a pleat in the towel alongside the first loaf, to separate the two loaves, and lay the second in place.

Final Rise Before Baking. Usually 1 to 1½ hours. Cover both loaves with the floured towel and let rise until more than doubled in volume. Meanwhile, make everything ready for baking, so that you may proceed almost at once.

EQUIPMENT NEEDED FOR BAKING FRENCH BREAD. French bread not only rises free-form, but it bakes free-form— not in a pan. It is difficult, even frustrating

to attempt it without the proper equipment. Here is what you will need.

A Hot Baking Surface. French bread does not cook properly when baked on a metal sheet. It must be slid upon a baking stone or a pizza stone, or line your oven rack with ceramic quarry tiles—available in some cookware shops or in building-supply stores.

Unmolding and Sliding Boards. The risen loaf is unmolded from its floured towel and slid onto the hot baking surface. I use ⅜-inch plywood bought at the home-improvement store, an 8-by-20-inch board for unmolding and for sliding a single loaf, and a 20-inch board 2 inches narrower than the width of my oven for sliding several long loaves or rolls.

Cornmeal. A light dusting of coarse cornmeal on the sliding board keeps the dough from sticking.

Steam. To prolong the rise and set the crust, you need steam the first few seconds of baking. In an electric oven, toss ½ cup water into the bottom, just before closing the door. In a gas oven, set a hot cast-iron frying pan on the lowest level as you preheat, and toss the water into that when the time comes.

To Bake 2 Loaves of French Bread. Slide the oven rack onto the middle or lower-middle level, set the baking stone or tiles upon it, and preheat the oven to 450°F. Sprinkle the sliding board lightly with cornmeal, and have your unmolding board and instant-read thermometer at hand.

Remove the covering towel and place the unmolding board against the inside side of one loaf, lift the towel on the other side, and flip the loaf, its smooth side up, onto the board, then nudge the loaf onto one side of the sliding board. Repeat with the second loaf. Push the loaves so that the ends of each are at one end of the board.

With a razor blade held almost flat, make 3 slightly angled slashes in the top of each loaf. Open the oven door. Poise the sliding board so that the ends of the loaves are about 1 inch from the back of the oven, then quickly snatch the board out from under the loaves, depositing them on the hot surface. Immediately pour ½ cup water onto oven floor or hot pan (see box page 83). Close the door. Bake 20 minutes; reduce temperature to 400°F and bake 10 minutes more, until done (see box below). Remove and cool on a rack.

WHEN IS THE BREAD DONE? The loaves should feel light, they should make a pleasant thump when tapped, but they are not done until an instant-read thermometer, left in for several seconds, reads 200°F.

VARIATIONS

■ BAGUETTES. After the second rise, divide the dough into 3 equal pieces. Shape, roll, and stretch each into a thin (2-inch diameter) rope; let rise until more than doubled. Bake as for fat

loaves, but check for doneness 5 minutes after reducing heat to 400°F.

■ ROUND COUNTRY LOAF (OR LOAVES). After the second rise, turn the dough out onto a floured surface; deflate as described in the master recipe. Use all the dough for 1 large loaf, or divide in half for 2 smaller loaves.

Pat the dough into a disk. Lift one side and bring it almost over the other; rotate a quarter turn, and repeat 6 to 8 times, to make a thick cushion. Turn the dough over and rotate it between your palms, tucking the sides under as you go, to make a smooth, round loaf.

Turn the dough over, smooth side underneath. Pinch the edges together, set on a floured towel, and cover with another towel. (Repeat with the remaining dough, if you are making 2.)

Let rise until more than doubled. Prepare and preheat oven to 450°F as in the master recipe. Transfer the loaves smooth side up to the cornmeal-dusted sliding board. Slash the top with your razor in a decorative pattern, such as a crosshatch or a tree with branches. Slide into the oven, create steam, and bake as in the master recipe. Large loaves may need an additional 10 to 15 minutes at 375°F to finish baking.

■ BAKING IN A LOAF PAN. Butter a 2-quart loaf pan. Pat the dough into a rectangle slightly smaller than the pan. Fold in half lengthwise twice, as for long loaves, to form an even rectangle. Place seam down in pan, press flat into corners. Let rise until dough has doubled in volume.

Meanwhile, slide rack onto lower-third level, and preheat the oven to 450°F. Slash top of loaf lengthwise down the center with a razor, and bake for 20 minutes, then reduce temperature to 400°F. When done (see box, page 84), turn out of pan and cool on a rack.

▪ HARD FRENCH ROLLS. After its second rise, divide dough into 12 pieces. Fold each in half. One at a time (or 2 when you are an expert), rotate the dough under the palm of one hand to form a ball. Pinch undersides to seal, and set smooth side down on a lightly floured towel. Cover with a second towel and let rise until more than doubled.

Prepare and preheat the oven to 450°F, as in the master recipe. Arrange the rolls 3 or 4 at a time smooth side up at the end of your cornmeal-dusted sliding board. Slash each with a circular stroke around the side, or a cross on top. Slide onto baking stone and rapidly continue with the rest. Make steam as in the master recipe. Bake 15 to 20 minutes, then reduce temperature to 375°F and bake a few minutes more until done (see box, page 84).

MAKING AND KNEADING DOUGH BY HAND. If you prefer to make the dough entirely by hand, mix the ingredients in a bowl with a sturdy wooden spoon, then turn dough out onto a lightly floured work surface. For the first few minutes, pick it up with a scraper and slap it down roughly, and continue a number of times, until the dough begins to have body. Let rest 5 minutes. Then proceed to knead it with your hands as described in the box on page 82.

▪ PIZZA. For two 16-inch tomato pizzas. Set rack on the lower-middle level and preheat the oven and pizza stone to 450°F.

Form the dough into 2 smooth balls and let rest, covered. After 10 minutes, lightly flour a pizza paddle; flatten and stretch the dough into a thin disk on the paddle by rolling it out and pressing into shape with your fingers, or stretch and twirl it, professional-style, while supporting it on both your fists and twisting them apart—you'll have to see it done to do it!

Brush the top of the dough generously with olive oil, dust with ½ cup of grated hard cheese, and spread over 2 cups of fresh tomato sauce (page 30). Drizzle on more olive oil, sprinkle on ½ cup or so of grated mozzarella cheese; a sprinkle of thyme, oregano, or Italian herbs; and a little salt and pepper. Drizzle on more oil and another ½-cup dusting of grated hard cheese.

Slide onto hot baking stone and bake 10 to 15 minutes, or until top is bubbling, edges have puffed, and bottom is crisped. Prepare second pizza while first is baking.

Baking in the Bread Machine: White Sandwich Bread—*Pain de Mie*

It's not always easy to find good sandwich bread, and when I need just one loaf I enjoy using the bread machine. I don't bake it in the machine, because I don't like the look of the loaf, but it's neat and easy for mixing and rising. Here's my formula, made in any standard-size machine.

For an 8-cup fairly straight-sided loaf pan

Proof 2 teaspoons yeast, 1½ tablespoons tepid water, and a pinch of sugar in a cup (see box, page 81). Meanwhile, melt ½ stick roughly sliced unsalted butter in ½ cup milk, then cool it off by adding 1 cup cold milk. Pour into the container of the machine along with 2 teaspoons salt, 1½ teaspoons sugar, 3½ cups plain unbleached all-purpose flour, and the proofed yeast. Start the machine and follow directions for "dough." After its rise, remove the dough, flatten it, fold into 3, and return it to the machine for a second rise. Then the dough is ready to form and bake.

Either bake as in "Baking in a Loaf Pan" on page 84, or, for a flat-topped, evenly rectangular loaf, fill the buttered pan by no more than a third, and let rise to slightly more than double. (Form any extra dough into rolls or baby loaves.) Cover top of pan with buttered foil, and set in the lower-middle level of the preheated 425°F oven. Set a baking sheet on top of the pan, weighting it down with a 5-pound something, like a brick or a metal object.

Bake 30 to 35 minutes, until the dough has filled the pan and is browning well. Then uncover the pan and continue another 10 minutes or so, until the loaf comes easily out of the pan. The interior temperature should be 200°F.

TWO DESSERTS BASED ON BREAD

Apple Charlotte *Serves 10*

4 pounds firm apples that hold their shape when cooking, such as Golden Delicious, peeled and chopped into ½-inch pieces
⅔ cup clarified butter (see box, page 36)
½ cup either light- or dark-brown sugar
Grated peel of 1 lemon
Small pinch of powdered cinnamon
⅓ cup sieved apricot jam
2 tsp pure vanilla extract
3 Tbs dark Jamaican rum
13 slices firm home-style sandwich bread (previous recipe), crusts off
1 cup apricot glaze (see box, page 103)
1½ cups custard sauce (*crème anglaise*, page 78)

Sauté the apple pieces in 2 table-spoons of the butter for 2 to 3 minutes. Sprinkle on brown sugar and lemon peel and continue for 5 minutes or more, until the apples start to brown and caramelize. Stir in the cinnamon, apricot jam, vanilla, and rum, and sauté another 2 minutes or so, until apples have absorbed the liquid.

Set racks in middle and lower-middle levels and preheat the oven to 425°F. Arrange 4 slices of bread in a square on your work surface. Center a 6-cup straight-sided circular baking dish such as a charlotte on the square, and cut around the bottom to make a circle of bread in 4 pieces; reserve them. Cut a 2-inch circle from another slice, and reserve.

Heat 3 tablespoons of the butter in a frying pan and brown the reserved bread pieces, including the circle, on both sides. Then brown the trimmings. Butter the bottom of the baking dish and line with a circle of wax paper. Arrange the circle of sautéed bread pieces over it (but reserve the small circle). Halve all the remaining bread slices lengthwise. One by one, dip each piece in the remaining butter and arrange upright and slightly overlapping around the inside of the mold. Spoon layers of sautéed apples alternating with sautéed bread trimmings (which act as fillers) into the dish, letting the filling hump ¾ inch over the rim.

Set in the middle rack of the oven, and then slide a pan underneath to catch any juices. Bake for about 30 minutes, pressing down on apples several times with a spatula, until bread strips lining the sides have browned nicely.

Remove from oven and let rest at least 1 hour. Unmold onto a serving plate, paint top and sides with apricot glaze; center the small circle on top and glaze. Serve warm or cold, with the *crème anglaise* on page 78.

Cinnamon Toast Flan—a Bread Pudding *For a 6-cup baking dish 2 inches deep, serving 6 to 8*

4 Tbs softened unsalted butter
6 or 7 slices white sandwich bread, crusts left on
¼ cup sugar mixed with 2 tsp ground cinnamon
5 "large" eggs
5 egg yolks
¾ cup sugar
3¾ cups hot milk
1½ Tbs vanilla extract

Butter the bread slices on one side, using half the butter. Arrange them buttered side up on a broiling rack and sprinkle cinnamon sugar over each. Watching carefully, broil a few seconds, until sugar bubbles up. Cut each slice into 4 triangles. Smear the remaining butter inside the baking dish, and fill with the toast triangles, sugar side up.

Make a custard sauce (*crème anglaise*, page 78) with the eggs, yolks, sugar, milk, and vanilla, and pour half through a sieve over the toast. Let soak 5 minutes, then sieve on the remaining custard.

Place the dish in a roasting pan and set in the lower-middle of a preheated 350°F oven. Pour boiling water into the pan to come halfway up the baking dish. Bake for 25 to 30 minutes, keeping the water bath at just below the simmer.

It is done when a skewer plunged into the custard an inch from the side comes out clean.

Serve hot, at room temperature, or cold, accompanied with a fruit sauce or cut-up fresh fruits. (It will keep 2 days in the refrigerator.)

CRÊPES—PAPER-THIN FRENCH PANCAKES

Crêpes are easy indeed to make and are a most useful resource for simple but dressy main courses and desserts. What is helpful, too, is that you can make a good number while you are at it and freeze the extras, ready almost at once for many a quick meal.

MASTER RECIPE

All-Purpose Crêpes *For about twenty 5-inch or ten 8-inch crêpes*

1 cup instant-blending flour or all-purpose flour, scooped and leveled (see box, page 97)
²/₃ cup cold milk
²/₃ cup cold water
3 "large" eggs
¼ tsp salt
3 Tbs melted butter, plus more for brushing on pan

Mix all the ingredients smoothly in a blender or food processor, or with a whisk. Refrigerate 10 minutes if you've used instant flour, ½ hour or more if all-purpose. A rest allows the flour particles to absorb the liquid, making for a tender crêpe. Heat a nonstick frying pan with bottom diameter 5 to 8 inches until drops of water dance on it; brush lightly with melted butter. Pour in 2 to 3 tablespoons of batter and tilt pan in all directions to cover bottom evenly. Cook about 1 minute, or until browned on the bottom; turn and cook briefly on the other side. Cool on a rack as you continue with the rest. When thoroughly cool, stack and refrigerate for 2 days, or freeze for several weeks.

ROLLED CRÊPES: SAVORY AND DESSERT ROULADES

Savory Spinach and Mushroom Crêpe Roulades

For 8 crêpes, serving 4. Prepare 2 cups béchamel sauce (page 13); 1¼ cups chopped, cooked, well-seasoned spinach (page 25); 1 cup quartered sautéed mushrooms (page 31). Spread a thin layer of sauce over the bottom of a buttered gratin dish and sprinkle with 2 tablespoons grated Swiss cheese. Mix spinach and mushrooms with ½ cup of sauce and divide into 8. Spoon 1 portion on the lower underside of each of 8 crêpes. Roll up the crêpes and arrange, seam down, in the dish. Spoon remaining sauce over them and sprinkle on another ½ cup of grated cheese. Bake in the upper third of a preheated 375°F oven for 25 to 30 minutes, just until bubbling and lightly browned on top.

Strawberry Dessert Crêpes

For 8 crêpes, serving 4. Mix a pint or more fresh sliced strawberries with a teaspoon or two each of sugar and kirsch, orange liqueur, or cognac, and let stand for an hour. Drain, spoon berries generously over the lower underside of a crêpe, and roll up. Arrange 2 crêpes, seam down, on each serving plate. Drizzle over a spoonful of berry juices and top with lightly whipped cream—*crème Chantilly* (page 101).

LAYERED CRÊPES: SAVORY AND DESSERT GÂTEAUX

Savory Tower of Crêpes with Lobster, Broccoli, and Mushrooms

For 10 to 12 crêpes, serving 5 to 6. Stir ½ cup of grated Swiss cheese into 2 cups warm béchamel sauce (page 13), making it now a Mornay sauce. Prepare 2 cups of creamed lobster (see box, page 66), using ½ cup of the sauce instead of heavy cream. Mix ½ cup of sauce into 2 cups of broccoli florets (page 25), and another ½ cup of sauce with 2 cups of quartered sautéed mushrooms (page 31).

Center a large crêpe in a baking dish and spoon on half of one filling; cover with another crêpe and half of second filling; top with a crêpe and half of the third filling. Repeat, ending with a plain crêpe, and spooning the remaining sauce over all.

Bake for 30 minutes in a preheated 400°F oven, or until bubbling and lightly browned.

Dessert Gâteau of Crêpes à la Normande

For 12 crêpes, serving 5 to 6. Spread 4 to 5 cups peeled and sliced Golden Delicious apples in a large baking pan; sprinkle over them ⅓ cup sugar and 4 tablespoons melted butter. Bake in a 350°F oven for 15 minutes, or until apples are tender. Center a small crêpe in a buttered baking dish, cover with a layer of apple slices, and sprinkle over it a tablespoon of macaroon crumbs, drops of melted butter, and drops of cognac. Lay a crêpe on top, then another apple-macaroon layer; repeat until you have 10 or 11 layers. Top with a final crêpe. Sprinkle melted butter and sugar over the top, and bake in a 375°F oven until bubbling hot.

OTHER FILLINGS.

For Savory Crêpes. Use any of the fillings and sauces suggested for omelets on pages 65–66.

For Dessert Crêpes. One of the simplest, and always popular as a family treat, is to spread the undersides with soft butter, sprinkle on sugar, roll them up, sprinkle sugar on top, and bake at 375°F until hot through. Serve as is, or flame them with cognac or orange liqueur. Or roll them up with apricot, strawberry, or raspberry jam; or orange marmalade; or the marvelous orange butter used for the following crêpes Suzette.

Crêpes Suzette *For 12 crêpes, serving 6*

2 fresh, firm, bright-skinned oranges
½ cup plus 1 Tbs sugar
2 sticks (8 ounces) unsalted butter
3 Tbs orange liqueur for the butter, plus
    ¼ cup for flaming
About ½ cup strained orange juice
12 crêpes (5-inch crêpes, see page 88)
¼ to ⅓ cup cognac

Peel the zest (orange part of peel only) from the oranges and pulverize in a food processor with the ½ cup sugar. Add the butter; when creamed, dribble in the 3 Tbs orange liqueur and the orange juice. In a large chafing dish or skillet, boil the orange butter for 4 or 5 minutes, until syrupy. One at a time, rapidly bathe crêpes in the butter; fold in half, best side out, and in half again, to form a wedge shape.

Arrange attractively in the chafing dish and sprinkle on the 1 tablespoon of sugar. Pour the remaining orange liqueur and the cognac into a ladle, then pour over the crêpes. When bubbling, tilt pan into the flame or light with a match and spoon the flaming liquid over the crêpes. Serve on very hot plates.

■ CRÊPES WITH ORANGE-ALMOND
BUTTER. Beat ½ cup finely ground
almonds or macaroon crumbs and ¼
teaspoon almond extract into the preceding
orange butter. Spread on 18 small
crêpes, fold them into wedges, and
arrange, overlapping, on a baking dish.
Sprinkle over them 3 tablespoons sugar
and heat in a 375°F oven for 15 minutes,
or until tops of crêpes begin to
caramelize. Pour ⅓ cup each orange
liqueur and cognac into a small saucepan,
heat, and ignite with a match. Spoon
flaming liquid over crêpes, and serve.

TARTS

Except for making the pie-crust dough, tarts are among the easiest of our culinary treasures
to produce, and the food processor makes that production even easier. Of course you can
buy ready-made pie shells, but it is a shame not to have the know-how yourself.

KEEP IT CHILLED! Dough with a high fat content like this one softens quickly at room
temperature and becomes difficult if not impossible to work with. Whenever this happens
to you, stop where you are and refrigerate it for 20 minutes. To make things easier for
me, I bought a marble slab that now lives in the refrigerator; I take out that chilled slab
and use it as a work surface any time I'm doing a dough.

MASTER RECIPE

All-Purpose Pie Dough—*Pâte Brisée Fine* Dough for two 9-inch round shells or a 14-by-18-inch free-form shell

You will note the mixture of flours and
fats here. Without them, our general
American all-purpose flour, which is relatively high in gluten, can give you a brittle
rather than a tender crust. But if you have
"pastry flour," you can use that alone,
along with all butter rather than a mixture
of butter and vegetable shortening.

1½ cups unbleached all-purpose flour
(measured by the scoop-and-level system; see box, page 97)
½ cup plain bleached cake flour
1 tsp salt
1½ sticks (6 ounces) chilled unsalted
butter, diced
4 Tbs chilled vegetable shortening
½ cup ice water, plus droplets more if
needed

Drop the flours, salt, and butter in
to the bowl of a food processor fitted
with the steel blade. Pulse 5 or 6 times
in ½-second bursts to break up the butter.

Then add the shortening, turn on the machine, and immediately pour in the ice water, pulsing 2 or 3 times. Remove cover and observe the dough, which will look like a mass of smallish lumps and should just hold in a mass when a handful is pressed together. If too dry, pulse in droplets more water.

Turn dough out onto your work surface, and with the heel of your hand rapidly and roughly push egg-size blobs out in front of you in 6-inch smears. Gather the dough into a relatively smooth cake; wrap in plastic, and refrigerate at least 2 hours (or up to 2 days), or you may freeze it for several months.

WHAT TO BAKE IT IN OR ON. Bake your tart shell in a bottomless buttered flan ring set on a buttered pastry sheet, or in a false-bottomed cake pan or fluted pan, or on a buttered upside-down pie plate or cake pan. Or you can fashion a free-form shell on a buttered pastry sheet.

VARIATION

■ SWEET DOUGH FOR DESSERT TARTS. Use the same formula, but cut the salt down to ¼ teaspoon and include 2 tablespoons sugar.

Forming a Tart Shell

To Form a 9-Inch Round Shell in a Flan Ring. Have the ring and pastry sheet buttered and at your side. Cut the chilled dough in half and keep one half

wrapped and chilled. Rapidly, on a lightly floured surface, roll the other half into a circular shape ⅛ inch thick and 1½ inches larger all around than your ring.

Roll the dough up on your pin and unroll it over the ring, then lightly press the dough in place. To make sturdy sides, push about ½ inch down them all around. Roll your pin over the top to trim off excess dough, then push it up ⅓ inch all around the sides to make a rim.

Using the tines of a table fork, laid flat, press a design on the rim. Prick the bottom of the dough all over with a fork. Cover with plastic wrap and chill at least 30 minutes before baking.

A PROPER ROLLING PIN. Get yourself a straight rolling pin about 18 inches long and 1¾ inches in diameter, or use an Italian pasta pin.

To Form a Shell on an Upside-Down Pan. Butter the outside of the pan and set it upside down on a baking sheet. Roll out the dough, drape loosely over the pan, and press gently onto pan all around. To make the wall thicker, push dough up on the sides with your thumbs. Press a decorative edging around the sides with the tines of a fork held flat.

To Form a Large Free-Form Rectangular Tart Shell. Roll the chilled dough into a 16-by-20-inch rectangle ⅛ inch thick. Roll it up on your pin and unroll onto a lightly buttered rimless baking sheet. Trim the sides perfectly straight, then slice a strip of dough 1 inch wide from each edge of the rectangle. Moisten the outside border of the rectangle with cold water and lay the strips on top to form a raised rim. Press the strips with the tines of a fork to seal and decorate, and prick the bottom all over with the tines of the fork. Wrap and chill.

Prebaking a Shell—"Blind Baking"

You will always have a crisper crust for tarts baked with a filling when you prebake the shell first.

Slide rack into the lower-middle level, and preheat the oven to 450°F. For a quiche ring, false-bottomed pan, or free-form shell, butter the shiny side of a piece of foil several inches larger than your shell. Press it lightly, buttered side down, against the chilled tart shell on the bottom and sides. To prevent bottom from rising and sides from collapsing, pour in dry beans, rice, or aluminum "pie weights," being sure you also bank them against the sides.

Bake 10 to 15 minutes, until the bottom pastry is set but still soft. Remove foil and beans, prick the bottom again with a fork, and return to oven. For a partial cooking, bake 2 minutes or so more, until pastry just begins to color and to separate from the sides if in a ring. For a fully cooked shell, bake 4 or more minutes, until lightly browned.

MASTER RECIPE FOR SAVORY TART

Quiche Lorraine *For a 9-inch quiche, serving 6*

6 strips of crisply cooked bacon
A partially baked 9-inch tart shell (see above)
3 "large" eggs
About 1 cup cream
Salt, freshly ground pepper, and nutmeg

Preheat oven to 375°F. Break bacon into pieces and strew in shell. Blend the eggs with enough cream to make 1½ cups of custard, and blend in seasonings to taste. Pour into shell to within ⅛ inch of rim. Bake 30 to 35 minutes, or until puffed and browned. Unmold onto a round platter and serve warm or at room temperature.

QUICHE PROPORTIONS. Any quiche can be made with either heavy or light cream or with milk. The proportions always are 1 egg in a measuring cup plus milk or cream to the ½-cup level; 2 eggs and milk or cream to the 1-cup level; 3 eggs and milk or cream to the 1½-cup level; and so forth.

VARIATIONS

■ CHEESE AND BACON QUICHE.
Follow the master recipe, but sprinkle ½ cup grated Swiss cheese into shell before adding the custard, plus another spoonful on top before baking.

■ SPINACH QUICHE. Blend 1 cup cooked chopped, well-flavored spinach (page 25) into the custard. Sprinkle 2 tablespoons grated Swiss cheese into the bottom of the shell, pour in the custard, sprinkle more cheese on top, and bake as directed.

■ SHELLFISH QUICHE. Prepare the shellfish as described on page 66, but omit the cream. Spread into the pastry shell, pour in the custard, sprinkle on 3 tablespoons grated Swiss cheese, and bake as directed.

■ ONION AND SAUSAGE QUICHE. Spread 2 cups tenderly sautéed minced onions in the shell. Pour the custard over, arrange on top thinly sliced cooked Italian sausage and $1/4$ cup grated Swiss cheese. Bake as directed.

■ OTHER ADDITIONS. Use about a cup for a 9-inch shell. Just about anything edible can be quiche material, from cooked or canned salmon to tunafish, the broccoli florets on page 25, the pipérade on page 32, sliced sautéed white of leek, sautéed mushrooms or chicken livers, and so forth.

MASTER RECIPE

Apple Tart *For a 9-inch tart, serving 4 to 6*

A prebaked 9-inch tart shell (pages 91, 93)
Warm apricot glaze (see box, page 103)

2 or 3 firm apples (such as Granny Smith or Golden Delicious), halved, cored, peeled, and neatly sliced
2 Tbs sugar

Paint the bottom of the shell with apricot glaze. Arrange the apples in a decorative pattern, filling the shell; sprinkle over the sugar. Bake in the upper-middle level of a preheated 375°F oven for 30 to 35 minutes, until the apples are lightly colored and perfectly tender. Unmold onto a platter and paint top of apples with more apricot glaze. Serve warm or cold.

VARIATIONS

■ FREE-FORM APPLE TART. Form a 14-by-18-inch free-form tart shell as detailed on page 92. Sprinkle 2 tablespoons sugar in the shell. Peel, core, and slice 3 or 4 Golden Delicious apples, and arrange in neat rows of overlapping slices. Sprinkle over more sugar. Bake and glaze as in the master recipe.

■ PEAR TART. Use firm ripe pears, such as Bartletts, in either of the preceding apple tarts.

■ FRESH STRAWBERRY TART. Paint a fully baked 8- or 9-inch tart shell with warm red-currant glaze (see box, page 103). Arrange 1 quart of fresh hulled strawberries attractively, heads up, in the shell, and paint lightly with more glaze. Serve with whipped cream on the side.

■ PASTRY CREAM AND STRAWBER-
RIES. After glazing the bottom of the
tart shell, spread on a layer no more than
1/4 inch thick of pastry cream (page 79),
then arrange the strawberries on top and
complete the recipe.

■ OTHER IDEAS. Rather than
strawberries, use raspberries, blueber-
ries, or a mixture; include halved
seedless grapes and/or a sprinkling of
chopped nuts; or sliced fresh or canned
peaches, apricots, or pears; or halved
ripe figs. This is a great opportunity
for you to use your creative skills.

The Famous Upside-Down Apple
Tarte Tatin

For 6 servings. Provide yourself with a
heavy ovenproof 9-inch skillet and a third
to a half of the recipe for chilled pie dough
(page 91). Slide rack onto lower-middle
level and preheat oven to 425°F.

Slice the halves of 6 cored and
peeled Golden Delicious apples into 4
lengthwise wedges each, and toss with
the grated zest and juice of 1 lemon and
1/2 cup sugar. Drain after macerating
20 minutes.

Heat 6 tablespoons unsalted butter
in the frying pan over high heat; stir in 1
cup sugar, and cook until syrup bubbles
and turns caramel-brown.

Off heat, arrange a layer of apple
slices in a neat pattern on the caramel
coating, then arrange the rest of the
apples fairly neatly on top.

Return over moderately high heat
and cook for about 25 minutes, covering
the pan after 10 minutes, and pressing
down on apples every several minutes as
you baste them with exuded juices.
When the juices are thick and syrupy,
remove from heat.

Roll the chilled dough into a circle,
3/16 inch thick and 1 inch larger than top
of pan. Drape over apples, pressing edge
of dough between apples and inside of
pan; cut 4 small steam holes on top.
Bake about 20 minutes, until the pastry
has browned and crisped.

Unmold onto a serving dish so the
pastry is on the bottom, and serve hot,
warm, or cold, with whipped cream, sour
cream, or vanilla ice cream.

TO CLEAN A BURN-BLACKENED PAN.
Fill the pan with water, adding 2 Tbs
baking soda per quart. Simmer 10
minutes, cover, and let soak off heat for
several hours or overnight. The black
residue should scrub off easily with a
stiff brush.

TIMING—REGULAR VERSUS CONVEC-
TION OVENS. All the timings in this
book are for regular ovens. Convection
ovens cook about one-third faster. In
other words, a leg of lamb that takes 2
hours at 325°F in a regular oven will
probably take less than 1 1/2 hours in a
convection oven.

Cakes and Cookies

"When you have mastered a number of frostings and fillings, cake making becomes just an assembly job."

You will find all the standard cake and cookie recipes detailed in numerous cookbooks, including some of mine. Here I am only touching on a few of my favorites, and spending more time on the fundamental "how-to"s, such as the beating of egg whites, the preparation of the cake pan, the measuring of flour, the melting of chocolate. Rather than giving two general cake recipes, I am concentrating on the *génoise,* that all-purpose work horse for layer cakes, petits fours, jelly rolls, cup cakes, and so forth. Before the electric mixer it was a real chore to make, since its basis is whole eggs and sugar beaten at length to produce a thick cream—arduous by hand, easier with a portable beater, easy indeed when you have one of the modern mixers on a stand. I have included a classic almond cake, a walnut cake, my favorite chocolate cake, and the always popular dacquoise with its crunchy meringue-nut layers. When you have a few cake formulas and filling ideas in your repertoire, you will find that it's pretty much an assembly job—you can mix and match a different way every time. Please note that there's only one cookie recipe—no more room!

CAKES

MASTER RECIPE

***Génoise* Cake** *For about 6 cups of batter, to make 1 round 9-by-1½-inch cake, or 1 round 8-by-2-inch cake (or enough for 16 cup cakes, or a 12-by-16-inch sponge sheet)*

½ cup plus ⅓ cup plain bleached cake flour (sifted and measured as per the box on page 97)
1 Tbs plus ½ cup sugar
¼ tsp salt
¼ cup warm clarified butter (see box, page 36)

4 "large" eggs
1 tsp pure vanilla extract

Preheat oven to 350°F, slide rack onto the lower-middle level, and prepare your pan (see box, page 97). Sift the flour with the 1 Tbs sugar and salt and reserve the clarified butter in a 2-quart bowl. Beat the eggs in your mixer bowl with the remaining sugar and the vanilla until you have "formed the ribbon." At once, rapidly sift on and fold in a quarter of the flour, then half the rest of the flour, and finally the last of it. Fold a large plop of this cake batter into the clarified butter, then fold the butter-batter back into the remaining batter. Turn batter into prepared pan, filling it to no more than 1/4 inch of the rim. Bang lightly on work surface to deflate bubbles, and bake 30 to 35 minutes, until puffed, lightly browned, and showing a faint line of shrinkage from sides of pan. Let cool 20 minutes before unmolding onto a rack. Let cool completely before filling and icing.

VARIATIONS

■ SERVING SUGGESTION: WHITE MOUNTAIN CHOCOLATE-FILLED GÉNOISE. Prepare a double amount of the Italian meringue on page 102, and flavor half of it with chocolate, as directed. Using a long, serrated knife, cut the cake in half horizontally. Place bottom half on a rack set over a tray, and turn the top half cut side up. Sprinkle both surfaces with rum-flavored imbibing syrup (see box, page 101), and spread the chocolate meringue over the bottom half. Turn the top half cut side down over the filling, and frost the cake with the remaining white Italian meringue. Before serving, dust with a sprinkling of grated chocolate.

TO PREPARE THE CAKE PAN. Smear inside bottom and sides lightly with softened butter. Cut a sheet of wax paper to fit bottom exactly, press it in place, and butter it. Pour 1/4 cup cake flour into pan, shake and turn in all directions to cover surface completely, turn pan upside down, and bang out excess flour.

TO MEASURE FLOUR: "THE SCOOP AND LEVEL SYSTEM." To avoid trouble, especially when making pastries, measure your flour accurately. For every recipe in this book, place the dry-measure cup on a large piece of wax paper. Scoop the flour directly into the sifter, and sift it directly into the cup until overflowing, then, using the flat edge of a big knife, sweep off excess flour level with the rim.

TO STORE A PLAIN CAKE. When thoroughly cool, refrigerate in an airtight plastic bag for several days, or freeze for several weeks.

■ CUP CAKES. Use the preceding génoise batter for cup cakes, following directions for almond cup cakes on page 98, which are some of my favorites with fruit desserts and tea.

■ JELLY ROLL—ROULADE. Preheat oven to 375°F and set rack in lower middle. Grease the inside of an 11-by-17-inch jelly-roll pan with soft butter and line with a sheet of wax paper, leaving an extra 2 inches of it at each end; butter the paper where it lines the pan. Roll flour in the pan to cover inside and knock out excess. Spread in the *génoise* batter and bake about 10 minutes, until cake is lightly colored and top feels springy. Remove from oven. The following maneuvers are to prevent cake from cracking. Slice off ¼ inch from each end of cake. Sprinkle top with confectioners' sugar. Cover with a sheet of wax paper and a slightly dampened towel. Set a tray over the top and reverse the two. Holding an end of the wax paper, lift off the jelly-roll pan. Then, very carefully, peel off the wax-paper backing. Sift a ⅛-inch layer of confectioners' sugar over the cake and roll it up in the damp towel; you may refrigerate it for a day or two. If frozen, be sure it has thoroughly defrosted before unrolling.

Serving Suggestion: Apricot Roulade. Unroll the cake, sprinkle with imbibing syrup (see box, page 101), spread on the apricot filling (page 103), and frost with meringue butter cream (page 102).

The Genoa Almond Cake— *Pain de Gênes*

A special almond cake. For a 9-by-1½-inch 6-cup round cake pan. Preheat oven to 350°F, and prepare the cake pan (see box, page 97). Measure out ⅓ cup all-purpose flour and return to sifter. Prepare ¾ cup pulverized blanched almonds (see box, page 105), and cream 1 stick unsalted butter in a mixing bowl until soft and fluffy. Meanwhile, beat 3 "large" eggs "to the ribbon" (see box, page 100) with ¾ cup sugar, 2 teaspoons

pure vanilla extract, and ¼ teaspoon almond extract. Fold 3 spoonfuls of the egg-sugar mixture into the creamed butter. Then fold sprinklings of flour alternating with spoonfuls of pulverized almonds into the mixture and, when almost absorbed, fold in the butter by scoopfuls. Turn into the prepared pan, bang lightly on work surface, and bake in the middle level of the oven about 30 minutes. Let cool 20 minutes before unmolding on a rack. When cold, either serve as is, sprinkled with confectioners' sugar, or split in two horizontally and fill with something like the brandy-butter on page 103, and top with glace royale (page 103).

FOLDING. Folding egg whites or flour or whipped cream or anything else into anything like a cake batter is an essential part of soufflé and cake making. You have to incorporate the one into the other without deflating the puff of the one or the other. To do so, plunge a large rubber spatula like a knife down into the center of the mixture, and draw it to the side of the bowl and up to the surface in a rapid scoop, bringing some of the bottom up over the top. Rotate the bowl slightly, and continue rapidly and gently for several scoops, until the elements are blended—but do not overdo it and deflate the puff.

■ ALMOND CUP CAKES. For 10 cup cakes baked in muffin tins of $1/3$-cup capacity. For easy unmolding, grease the tins with a paste of 2 tablespoons flour and 2 tablespoons clarified melted butter. Divide the cake batter among the tins and bake about 15 minutes at 350°F, or until puffed and lightly browned. Let cool 15 minutes before unmolding. When cool, top with confectioners' sugar or the white glace-royale icing in the box on page 103.

Le Brantôme—a Walnut Layer Cake

Another cake with nuts. For two 9-inch cakes layered together, serving 10 to 14. Preheat oven to 350°F, prepare cake pans, and pulverize 1 cup walnut meats. Sift $1½$ cups all-purpose flour with 2 teaspoons double-action baking powder and return to sifter (see box, page 97). Whip $1½$ cups chilled heavy cream into soft mounds (see box, page 101). Finally, beat the eggs and sugar to "make the ribbon" (see box, page 100), gradually fold in two-thirds of the flour, scoop the whipped cream on top of the mixture, and fold it in along with sprinklings of the walnuts and the remaining flour. Turn the batter into the pans, and bake about 25 minutes in the middle level of the oven. Let cool 10 minutes before unmolding on racks. When thoroughly cool, fill and ice as described below.

Filled and Frosted Walnut Layer Cake. Set one of the walnut cakes on a circular rack over a tray and spread on top a good $1/4$-inch layer of filling, such as the brandy-butter on page 103. Turn the second cake upside down over the first and paint the top and sides of the structure with warm apricot glaze (see box, page 103). While the glaze is still warm, brush chopped walnuts around the walls of the cake and transfer to a serving platter. Spread a thin layer of glace-royale frosting (see box, page 103) over the top of the cake and decorate, if you wish, with walnut halves.

La Reine de Saba—the Queen of Sheba Chocolate Almond Cake

My favorite chocolate cake. For an 8-by-$1½$-inch cake, serving 6 to 8. Preheat oven to 350°F, set rack in lower-middle level, and prepare the cake pan. Measure out $½$ cup sifted plain bleached cake flour (see box, page 97) and $1/3$ cup blanched pulverized almonds (see box, page 105). Using an electric mixer, cream 1 stick unsalted butter with $½$ cup sugar; when fluffy, one at a time beat in 3 egg yolks. Meanwhile, melt 3 ounces semi-sweet chocolate and 1 ounce bitter choco-late with 2 tablespoons dark rum or strong coffee (see box, page 103), and stir the warm chocolate into the yolks. Beat 3 egg whites into stiff, shining peaks (see box, page 100), and stir a quarter of them into the yolks. Rapidly and delicately fold in the rest, alternating with sprinklings of almonds and siftings of flour. Turn at once into the prepared pan and bake about 25 minutes, until it has puffed to the top of the pan but the center moves slightly when gently shaken.

Let cool 15 minutes before unmolding. This type of chocolate cake is always at its best at room temperature. Serve with a dusting of confectioners' sugar, or with the soft chocolate icing on page 102.

PERFECTLY BEATEN EGG WHITES.

The Electric Mixer. Whether you are using a mixer on a stand or a hand-held mixer, use a round-bottomed glass, stainless-steel, or unlined copper bowl just wide enough to hold the mixer blade or blades, so that the entire mass is in continuous motion as you beat. This is essential for beating egg whites—as well as for beating whole eggs and sugar. (If you do any serious cooking, you'll never regret investing in a professionally designed heavy-duty electric mixer. It costs money but it really does the work, and it will last you a lifetime.)

Preparing Beater and Bowl. To make sure the beating bowl and beater are absolutely grease-free, pour 1 tablespoon of vinegar and 1 teaspoon of salt into the bowl and rub clean with a paper towel, then rub the beater with the towel. Do not rinse, since the trace of vinegar will help stabilize the egg whites. Be sure there is no trace of egg yolk in the whites.

Beating. If the eggs are chilled, set bottom of bowl in hot water for a minute or so to warm briefly to room temperature. Whip them fast for 2 or 3 seconds,

just to break them up, then start slow and gradually increase speed to fast, watching very carefully not to overbeat if you have a powerful mixer. They are done when a bit is lifted up in the wires of the beater and it forms a stiff, shining peak, bending down slightly at the tip.

Beating Whole Eggs and Sugar "to the Ribbon." The same general principles apply—the beater/bowl relationship, grease-free equipment, and warming the eggs over hot water if chilled. Beat 4 to 5 minutes or more, until they are thick and pale and a bit dropped from the beater forms a fat, slowly dissolving ribbon on the surface.

Meringue-Nut Layer Cakes— Dacquoise

Easier to make than conventional cakes, these are always immensely popular with guests. For 3 layers, 4 by 16 inches and 3/8 inch thick. Preheat oven to 250°F, and place racks in upper- and lower-third levels. Butter the surfaces of 2 baking sheets, dust with flour, and shake off excess, then mark on them three 4-by-16-inch rectangles. Pulverize 1½ cups toasted almonds or hazelnuts (be sure they are fresh!) with 1½ cups sugar and reserve. Beat ¾ cup (5 to 6) egg whites with a big pinch of salt and ¼ teaspoon cream of tartar to soft peaks (see box above), and continue beating as you add 1 tablespoon pure vanilla extract and ¼ teaspoon almond extract and sprinkle in 3 tablespoons sugar. Beat to stiff, shining peaks. (This is now a Swiss meringue, which you could also turn into individual baked meringues.). By big sprinkles, rapidly fold in the pulverized nuts and sugar. Using a pastry bag, fill the 3 rectangles on the baking sheets. Immediately set in the oven and bake about an hour, switching levels every 20 minutes. They should barely color, and are done when you can push them loose. If not used within a few hours, wrap airtight and store in the freezer.

SERVING SUGGESTION

■ CHOCOLATE HAZELNUT DACQUOISE. Trim and even the edges of the layers with a serrated knife, and paint tops of each with apricot glaze (see box, page 103). Layer with chocolate-ganache (page 102) or chocolate-meringue filling (page 102), bringing it up and around the cake. Brush chopped nuts around the sides of the cake, and strew a decorative layer of shaved or grated chocolate on top. Cover and refrigerate for several hours, to soften the meringue and set the filling, but bring back almost to room temperature before serving.

TO WHIP CREAM. For about 2 cups of softly whipped cream—*crème Chantilly*. Pour 1 cup of chilled heavy cream into a metal bowl set over a larger bowl of ice and water. To incorporate as much air as possible, either sweep a large balloon whip down and around and up into the bowl with rapid strokes, or circulate a hand-held electric mixer with vigorous movements.

The cream will not begin to thicken for several minutes. It is done when the beater leaves light traces on the surface and the cream holds softly when lifted.

IMBIBING SYRUP—FLAVORING AND MOISTENING FOR LAYER CAKES. Makes about 1 cup, enough for 3 cake layers. Stir $1/3$ cup hot water into $1/4$ cup sugar; when dissolved, stir in $1/2$ cup cold water and 3 to 4 tablespoons white rum, orange liqueur, or cognac or 1 tablespoon pure vanilla extract. Sprinkle over each cake layer before spreading on the filling.

SUGAR BOILING FOR SYRUPS AND CARAMEL. Proportions are always $1/3$ cup water for every 1 cup of sugar.

Simple Syrup. For imbibing cake layers, for instance. Stir over heat until sugar has completely dissolved.

The Thread Stage. Used for butter creams and Italian meringue. When the sugar has dissolved completely, cover the pan tightly and boil over high heat—never stirring—until when you rapidly take up a little in a metal spoon the last drops to fall from its tip into a cup of cold water form threads.

Caramel. Continue boiling until bubbles are thick, then uncover the pan, swirl it slowly by its handle, and boil until the syrup has darkened into caramel. Pour at once into a separate pan to stop the cooking.

To Clean Pans and Spoons. Fill pan with water, add tools, and simmer a few minutes to melt the syrup.

FILLINGS AND FROSTINGS

Here is another vast subject; I am only touching on the essentials. The glorious but tricky butter cream, with its egg-yolk base, was the standard frosting and filling of classic pastry, but in modern times the equally delicious but far simpler ganache, consisting only of melted chocolate and heavy cream, has largely taken its place when chocolate is called for. Again, you will find recipes for all of the classics in other cookbooks, including some of mine.

Italian Meringue

To be used as a frosting and filling and as an accompaniment. Enough to frost a 9-inch cake. Beat ²/₃ cup (4 to 5) egg whites with ¹/₄ teaspoon cream of tartar and a pinch of salt to soft peaks (see box, page 100) and turn machine to slow. Meanwhile, boil 1¹/₂ cups sugar and ¹/₂ cup water to the thread stage (see box, page 101). Beating the eggs at moderate speed, slowly dribble in the hot syrup. Increase speed to moderately fast and continue beating until the meringue is cool and forms stiff, shining peaks.

VARIATIONS

■ MERINGUE BUTTER CREAM FILLING. For a 9-inch cake. Cream 1 stick of unsalted butter until light and fluffy, then fold in 1 to 1¹/₂ cups of Italian meringue. Season with 1 teaspoon of white rum or orange liqueur, or 2 teaspoons of pure vanilla extract.

■ CHOCOLATE MERINGUE FILLING. For a 9-inch cake. Fold 4 ounces of tepid, smoothly melted semisweet chocolate

into the preceding meringue butter cream, and flavor with 2 tablespoons dark rum.

LEFTOVERS. May be refrigerated for several days, or frozen for several months.

■ MERINGUE CREAM FILLING. To fill a 9-inch cake. Combine 1 cup of Italian meringue with 1 cup of softly whipped cream (see box, page 101), and flavor as suggested for the butter cream.

Chocolate Ganache

To frost a 9-inch cake. Bring 1 cup heavy cream to the simmer in a 1¹/₂-quart saucepan. Lower heat and stir in 8 ounces semisweet chocolate broken into bits. Stir briskly until melted and smooth, then remove from heat. It will thicken as it cools.

Soft Chocolate Icing

For an 8-inch cake. Melt 2 ounces semisweet chocolate with 1 ounce bitter chocolate, a pinch of salt, and 1¹/₂ tablespoons rum or strong coffee (see box). When smooth and glistening, beat in by spoonfuls 6 tablespoons softened unsalted butter. Stir over cold water until cooled to spreading consistency.

Brandy-Butter Cake Filling

For a 9-inch cake. Beat 1 egg over moderate heat in a small saucepan with 3 tablespoons cognac, 2 tablespoons unsalted butter, 1/2 tablespoon cornstarch, and 1 cup sugar. Boil slowly 2 to 3 minutes to cook the starch, remove from heat, and beat in 2 to 4 table-spoons additional butter. The filling will thicken as it cools.

Apricot Filling

Enough for a 9-inch, 3-layer cake. Pour the contents of three 17-ounce cans of unpeeled apricot halves into a sieve set over a saucepan. When well drained, chop apricots and set aside. Boil the apricot juice with 3 tablespoons unsalted butter, 1/2 teaspoon cinnamon, 1/3 cup sugar, and the grated zest and strained juice of 1 lemon. When thick and syrupy, stir in the chopped apricots and boil several minutes, stirring until thick enough to hold its shape softly in a spoon.

TO MELT CHOCOLATE

Chocolate Melted with Liquid Flavoring. Always use the proportion of a minimum of 1 tablespoon liquid per every 2 ounces chocolate. For 1 1/2 cups. Break into small pieces 6 ounces semisweet chocolate and 2 ounces bitter chocolate, place in a small pan, and add 1/4 cup dark rum or strong coffee. Bring 3 to 4 inches water to the boil in a larger pan, remove from heat, cover the chocolate pan, and set it in the hot water. In 4 to 5 minutes the chocolate should have melted; stir to smooth it.

Melting Plain Chocolate. Use the same system, but do not let any liquid near it. Or, for large amounts, cover the chocolate pan and set in a 100°F oven, where it will melt smoothly in about half an hour.

The Microwave. I don't use it for chocolate—too risky.

FRUIT GLAZES FOR CAKES AND TARTS

Apricot Glaze. Sieve 1 cup of apricot jam, blend with 3 tablespoons sugar and, if you wish, 3 tablespoons dark rum, and boil it down until the last drops to fall from the spoon are thick and sticky. Use while warm.

Red Currant Glaze. Make the same way, using 1 1/4 cups unsieved red currant jelly and 2 tablespoons sugar.

GLACE ROYALE—WHITE SUGAR ICING FOR THE TOPS OF CAKES AND COOKIES. Using a hand-held electric mixer, beat 1 egg white in a small mixing bowl with 1/4 teaspoon lemon juice and 1 cup sifted confectioners' sugar. Beat in 1 teaspoon pure vanilla extract, then slowly add up to about 1 cup more confectioners' sugar, until you have a smooth, thick white paste that stands up in peaks. This

will take several minutes of beating. If not used almost at once, cover with a slightly dampened paper towel.

COOKIES

Only one cookie! But a most useful one, since you can serve it not only as a cookie but as a liner for molded desserts, and you can turn the batter into a sweet container. Make a lot while you are at it, since they freeze perfectly.

Cat's Tongues—*Langues de Chat, Finger-Shaped Sugar Cookies*

For about 30 4-by-1¼-inch cookies. Preheat oven to 425°F and set racks in upper- and lower-middle levels. Butter and flour 2 or more baking sheets (see box, page 97), and insert a ⅜-inch round tube into your pastry bag. Briefly beat 2 "large" egg whites in a small bowl to blend, and set aside. Using a portable electric mixer, cream ½ stick of unsalted butter in another bowl with ⅓ cup sugar and the grated rind of 1 lemon. When soft and fluffy, start folding in the egg whites rapidly, with a rubber spatula, ½ tablespoon at a time. Do not overdo. Keep the mixture puffed and fluffy.

Then, by big sprinkles, delicately and rapidly fold in ⅓ cup all-purpose flour. Turn the batter into the pastry bag and form shapes 4 inches by ½ inch spaced 3 inches apart on the baking sheets. Bake 2 sheets at a time for 6 to 8 minutes, until an ⅛-inch border around the edges of each cookie has browned.

Remove from oven and at once, with a flexible-blade spatula, dislodge cookies onto a rack. They crisp as they cool.

VARIATIONS

▮ COOKIE CUPS. These make charming edible containers. For 8 cups 3½ inches across. Preheat oven to 425°F and set rack in middle or lower-middle level. Lightly oil the outside of 2 large teacups (or bowls or jars that flare out) and turn upside down. Butter and flour 2 baking sheets (see box, page 97), and mark four 5½-inch circles spaced 2 inches apart on each. Prepare the preceding cookie batter and, one sheet at a time, drop a spoonful of batter in the center of each circle. Spread out to ¹/₁₆-inch thickness with the back of a spoon. Bake about 5 minutes, until cookies have browned to within an inch of the center. Set baking sheet on the open door of the oven. Immediately and rapidly, remove one cookie at a time with a flexible-blade spatula, turn it upside down over one of the teacups, and press into place. It will crisp almost at once. Proceed with the second cookie, remove the first from the cup to a rack, and proceed quickly with the third, then the fourth. Close the oven door to bring temperature back up to 425°F before continuing with the second sheet. (Cookies will keep a day or two in a closed container, or can be frozen.)

Serving Suggestions: Fill with ice cream, sherbet, fresh berries, or a dessert mousse.

◪ TUILES. Rather than being flat, these are curved, like a roof tile. Form the cookies on a rolling pin or bottle, to make a curved shape. Or wrap them around the handle of a wooden spoon for cylinders, or around a cornucopia shape, and fill with something like a sweet raspberry mousse.

TO PULVERIZE ALMONDS AND OTHER NUTS. Grind up to ½ cup at a time in an electric blender with on-off pulses, or up to ¾ cup in a food processor, always adding at least 1 tablespoon of granulated sugar to prevent the nuts from turning oily.

◪ ANOTHER FORMULA WITH GROUND NUTS: *TUILES AUX NOIX*— ALMOND OR HAZELNUT WAFERS. Use exactly the same formula as for the cat's tongues, but fold into the creamed butter 1 cup of toasted and ground hazelnuts or almonds and 2 tablespoons heavy cream. Then proceed to incorporate the egg whites, and finally the flour.

P. S. BISCUITS

I forgot the biscuits! You can't have a cookbook, however short it is, without a proper recipe for baking-powder biscuits, and you can't have a proper strawberry shortcake without them, either. Just before putting the proofs for this book to bed, David Nussbaum and I worked this out in Judith Jones's Northeast Kingdom Vermont kitchen.

Baking-Powder Biscuits

When the talk is about biscuits I always think of Leah Chase, chef and owner of Dookie Chase's in New Orleans, and those she baked for us on one of our *Master Chef* TV programs. They were the tenderest, the lightest, and really the best I ever remember eating. This is our interpretation of her method. The key to tender biscuits is using light, rapid movements, so that you activate the gluten in the flour as little as possible, and the flour itself plays a role. Southerners make their famous biscuits with soft wheat (low gluten) flour, and to approach its equivalent use part regular all-purpose and part cake flour as indicated here.

For about 1 dozen 2½-inch biscuits, baked in a 425°F oven. Preheat the oven. Provide yourself with a pastry blender or 2 knives, a pastry sheet either covered with parchment paper or buttered and floured as described on page 97, and a round 2½-inch cookie cutter.

Measure into a large mixing bowl either 1½ cups unbleached all-purpose flour and ½ cup plain bleached cake flour or 2 cups soft wheat (pastry) flour, plus 1⅔ tablespoons fresh lump-free double-action baking powder (see box, page 107), ¾ teaspoon salt, and 1 tablespoon sugar. Mix thoroughly then, with the pastry blender or 2 knives, rapidly cut in ¾ cup vegetable shortening (I use Crisco) until the flour-covered fat particles look like small peas. With a wooden spoon or your hands, lightly and rapidly, but in big dollops, fold in 1 cup of milk to make a rough, somewhat sticky, dough—do not attempt a smooth mixture at this point.

Turn the dough out onto a well-floured work surface and, as a gentle type of kneading, lift the far side up over onto the near side, pat it out gently into a fat circle, sprinkle on a little flour as necessary, then lift the left side over the right, the right over the left, and so forth, giving 6 folds in all. Finally spread and pat the dough into a reasonably smooth rectangle ¾ inch thick.

Cut out biscuit circles and place them close together, but not touching, on the pastry sheet. Gently gather the scraps together and give 2 or 3 folds as before, pat out again into a rectangle, cut out the circles and place them on the baking sheet, and continue until the dough is used up. Finally, pressing the sides of each biscuit shape with your fingers all around, plump them up slightly. Set in the middle or lower-middle of the preheated oven and bake for 15 to 20 minutes, or until cooked through and slightly browned.

Serve warm or at room temperature. (Leftovers, if any, are best frozen, then set from freezer for a few minutes into a 350°F oven.)

BAKING POWDER in an opened can loses its strength after about 6 months, so always test it by stirring a teaspoonful into 1/2 cup of hot water. If it doesn't bubble up in a lively way, throw it out. Before you use baking powder, be sure to smooth out any lumps.

VARIATION

■ STRAWBERRY SHORTCAKE. Use 2 tablespoons sugar rather than 1 in the dough, and you may prefer to form it into a single large cake 1 inch high. Plan on about 2 cups of fresh ripe strawberries per serving. Leaving one whole big fine berry for decoration, halve or quarter the rest, toss in a bowl with drops of fresh lemon juice and a good teaspoon or so of sugar for each quart. Let stand for 10 minutes or more, allowing the juices to exude. Toss again and add a little more lemon and sugar if needed. When it's time for dessert, split the biscuits (or single large cake) in half horizontally, spoon strawberries and their juices over the bottom halves, set on the tops, crown with a generous dollop of sweetened whipped cream (see box, below), center the reserved berry on top, and proudly serve. You may wish to pass around extra whipped cream separately.

SWEETENED WHIPPED CREAM. For 2 cups, whip 1 cup heavy cream or whipping cream as directed in the box on page 101. Just before serving, sift on 1/2 cup of confectioners' sugar and fold it in with a large rubber spatula, adding, if you wish, 1/2 teaspoon of pure vanilla extract.

Index

butterflied meat. *See* Chicken;
    Game Hens; Lamb; Pork;
    Poussins; Turkey
butterflying a chicken, 45

C

Cabbage
    about shredding, 22
    about steaming and serving, 27
    Cole Slaw, 22
    Red, Sweet and Sour, 34
Cake(s), 96–101. *See also* Filling and
    Frosting
    about, 96; storing, 97
    Chocolate Almond, The Queen of
      Sheba, 99
    Cup Cakes, 97
    Fruit Glazes for (Apricot, Red
      Currant), 103
    The Genoa Almond Cake—*Pain de
      Gênes,* 98; Almond Cup Cakes,
      99
    Génoise, 96; variations, 97–8
    imbibing syrup for flavoring and
      moistening layer cakes, 101; and
      Jelly Roll, 98
    Nut-Meringue Layer—Dacquoise,
      100; Chocolate Hazelnut, 101
    pans, about preparing, 97
    A Walnut Layer Cake—*Le Brantôme,*
      99
Calf's Liver and Onions, 42
canned broth (bouillon), soups made
    from, 6–8. *See also* Soup
Caramel Custard, 76–7; variations, 77

caramel and syrups, sugar boiling for,
    101
Carrot(s)
    about cooking and serving, 28
    Grated Sautéed/Steamed, 32
    Soup, Cream of, 10
Cat's Tongues—*Langues de Chat,*
    Finger-Shaped Sugar Cookies, 104;
      variations, 104–5
Cauliflower
    about steaming and serving, 27
    au Gratin, 31
celeriac. *See* Celery Root
Celery, Braised, 33
Celery Root Rémoulade, 22
Cheese
    and Bacon Quiche, 93
    Shirred Eggs Gratinéed with, 69
    Soufflé, Savory, 71–2;
      variations, 72–3
Chiboust (meringue pastry cream), 79
Chicken. *See also* Duck; Game Hens;
    Turkey
    about judging doneness of sauté, 44;
      roast, 54
    Blanquette of, 59
    Bonne Femme—Mushrooms, Onions,
      and Potatoes, 44
    Breast of, Served in a Salad, 19
    Breasts, Boneless, 40
    Broiled Butterflied, 45; variations,
      46
    butterflying, 45
    Chowder, 12
    French-Style Country Paté, 53
    Fricassee, 61
    giblets, about using, 54

H

I

A NOTE ABOUT THE AUTHOR

Julia Child was born in Pasadena, California. She graduated from Smith College and worked for the OSS during World War II in Ceylon and China. Afterward she and her husband, Paul, lived in Paris, where she studied at the Cordon Bleu, and taught cooking with Simone Beck and Louisette Bertholle, with whom she wrote the first volume of *Mastering the Art of French Cooking* (1961).

In 1963 Boston's WGBH launched the *French Chef* television series, which earned her the Peabody Award in 1965 and an Emmy in 1966. Her subsequent public television shows—*Julia Child & Company* (1978), *Julia Child & More Company* (1980), *Cooking with Master Chefs* (1993), *In Julia's Kitchen with Master Chefs* (1995), *Baking with Julia* (1996), and most recently her one-on-one collaboration with Jacques Pépin, *Julia and Jacques Cooking at Home* (1999)—have all been accompanied by books of the same names.

Ms. Child lives in Cambridge, Massachusetts, and Santa Barbara, California.

A NOTE ON THE TYPE

The text of this book was set in Scala, a typeface designed by Martin Majoor in 1988 for the Vrendenburg Music Centre in Utrech for use in their printed matter. Two years later FSI Fontshop International published FF Scala as the first serious text face in the then-new FontFont Library. In 1993 it was augmented with a sans-serif version, also released by FSI.

COMPOSED BY NORTH MARKET STREET GRAPHICS,
LANCASTER, PENNSYLVANIA

PRINTED AND BOUND BY R. R. DONNELLEY & SONS,
HARRISONBURG, VIRGINIA

PHOTOGRAPHS BY PAUL CHILD

DESIGNED BY CAROLE GOODMAN / BLUE ANCHOR